No fiction, no reporting, has yet captured what Mary Frances Greene and Orletta Ryan so vividly present in

THE SCHOOLCHILDREN.

This is the way life is in two New York public schools —one in Puerto Rican East Harlem and one in Harlem itself. The first part of this book carries the reader through a teacher's day, hour by hour. What is it like to teach children with overwhelming psychiatric problems, for whom no real help is offered? How do the children themselves react to the teacher's authority, to the disruptions in the classroom, to the irrelevant and often inadequate teaching program? And what do the teachers do about it? The second part of the book turns directly to the children, and here they speak for themselves. How do they feel? What is their home life? How are they really affected by poverty, mental illness, prejudice? Because it is based on actual conversations in the classroom, on the way the children express themselves, the book, while treating such agonizing questions, is constantly alive, moving . . . often even funny.

"Most Americans don't even know these conditions exist. The facts should shock the country."—America

"For those who have not walked through Harlem or Watts or Hough—this is what it sounds like—somebody should listen."—Virginia Kirkus

Other SIGNET Books of Special Interest

MANCHILD IN THE PROMISED LAND *by Claude Brown*
The provocative bestselling autobiography revealing
the spirit of a new pioneering generation of Negroes in
the North who have entered the mainstream of
American society as a determined, aggressive, hopeful
people. (#Q2938—95¢)

SLUMS AND SUBURBS *by James B. Conant*
The distinguished former President of Harvard attacks
the inequalities that exist between the public schools
of the slums and those of the wealthy suburbs.
(#P2421—60¢)

LETTERS FROM MISSISSIPPI *by Elizabeth Sutherland*
A moving record of an historic summer revealed
through the letters of young men and women who went
to live and work with Negro families in Mississippi
during the summer of 1964. (#T2943—75¢)

WHAT THEY ARE DOING TO YOUR CHILDREN
by Max Rafferty
A statement of the explosive views of the controversial
California educator, charging that progressive education has failed and that it is time to return to the old
system based on the three R's, discipline, competition,
and enlightened enquiry. (#T3009—75¢)

THE
SCHOOLCHILDREN

Growing Up in the Slums

Mary Frances Greene
and
Orletta Ryan

A SIGNET BOOK

Published by The New American Library

INTRODUCTION

This book is about schoolchildren of East Harlem and Harlem, in New York City. The two schools lie in the heart of the world's richest city, the center of arts and communication in our time. Both are the "special service" schools, schools in economically disadvantaged neighborhoods running on exceptionally high budgets, which now comprise a third of the New York system. Most of the fourth-grade children described in the book read on or about first-grade level. Several children in each class are nonreaders, and may still be nonreaders when they graduate into junior high—where two or three more pre-high school years may complete the only education most of them will ever receive.

In Memory of Rita Yvonne Ryan

Out of Ireland have we come.
Great hatred, little room
Maimed us at the start.
I carry from my mother's womb
A fanatic heart.

—WILLIAM BUTLER YEATS

Contents

PART I

East Harlem

Monday morning, 8:15. Teachers passing, gabbling in groups: ". . . so Saturday, Burt got in from college and from then *on*—" ". . . second inlay on the terrace but when the contractor finally got out to Jackson Heights, Joe'd read up on do-it-yourself and we decided—" ". . . so I told her, if we didn't get out there *this* week-end, it'd be gone. It was the most darling old Colonial pewter—" Hall guards, ladies with badges, are shoving children out the ——th Street entrance: "The bell ain't rung yet—" and children: "Screw you . . ."

At the stairway next to the office of Assistant Principal Zang, Edith, a beautiful woman of thirty-five from Barbados, is washing "pussy" and "f—— you" from the wall. Teachers swarm past her. Her long dark arm rises and falls patiently . . . she picks up the bucket, moves on. She does this every morning. Two policemen are knocking on Zang's door, and I follow them into the office. I too have to see Zang this morning about Danny Aguilez, an eleven-year-old who carries a compass that he uses on children and on Wednesday told me to f—— myself and threw a chair. With the help of a guard, Danny was dragged down to the office on Wednesday, where he repeated it, "f——ing bitch," in front of Zang and four others. Zang had heard of this kid before—Danny had been around the school for four years, progressively growing sicker. Zang said, "Can't we handle this tomorrow? . . ." But tomorrow never came for Mr. Zang.

Danny did not return to class, however; then the next Thursday afternoon he did appear, suddenly, alone, to terrorize the room before two grown men could remove him. Even now (I've had the boy twice before) he may be bounced back.

The office is mobbed. Clerks are yelling at teachers and

9

picking up phone calls from downtown about substitutes. Mrs. Rumstedt is waving pink and green terry-cloth washcloths—dogs or pussycats with little bars of soap in the ears—at teachers entering. "Take a couple, hon. They're just fifty cents and the money goes to the Nephritis Foundation. I'm doing this for my little niece—ohhh yes, she's got nephritis. You think I'd be doing this if she didn't? The children *in* the nephritis hospitals make them."

"Misser Zang not in," Zang's clerk tells the policemen and me, not moving a muscle except to turn back to her long-armed repose and a deep buddy-buddy talk she's having with Miss Skally. Skally talks everybody's language—favorite teacher with the clerks. "They're gahbage," she tells the clerks. "Real gahbage, some of these kids we have to work with here. . . ." Most of the high-screamy conversations are clustered around the mailboxes. The teachers ignore each other or else, swinging large bags very fast, prance up and down at each other, tugging or adjusting Kimberly knits, comparing body changes. "Look at that! Remember how it bulged a month ago? I went on lettuce and Metrecal, and—" Most of them hold M.A.'s in Education from Buffalo, Hunter, Bank Street. The air fills with chatter. Miss Flash, speech coordinator, who says "idears" and "bananers," greets me with furious enthusiasm. Iris Frost's box still loaded—she's still somewhat hung over. Someone saw her down the street in the luncheonette. She runs the health class; naps from one to two while the children nap, one has heard.

More teachers arriving. Husbands and taxicabs deposit passengers on the avenue sidewalk. Peals of laughter. A new late little group is hurrying in, talking of the week-end—dancing, Chinese dinners, and *Hello, Dolly!* Or a recount of a lonely week-end from one or two. They fly apart to dip separately into the crammed boxes, and Mrs. Moss is revealed waiting impatiently next to my box, for me. "What do you think of *this?*"

"Oh nice, Hazel. You really smell nice this morning."

"Thirty-two dollars an ounce. I'm a fool to be wearing it. But when I was married to that accountant, kid, I sweated it. I *found out*. With me the new thing is, 'Hazel, take care of yourself. No one else is going to.' I had *it*. Twenty years of it. From now on—"

Mr. Pickard, M.A. in European History from NYU, who teaches C.R.M.D. (Children of Retarded Mental Development) classes that bake bread and saw and hammer all day, comes up to start a big intellectual conversation which Skally's quick ear picks up from yards down the counter. Whatever it's about, she'll come over. She'll have read it, or done it, or thought of it and junked it *way* back. Skin diving? Oh yeah, she went in for that for a while. Someone's writing a book on slow learners? Oh, yeah, she thought of that but it would take time; there's really so much research when you get into that kind of thing. Camus? "Oh yeah, I read all that!" "Which of all that?" says Pickard, who's backed up to the door to airplane his notices into the basket. "Just what I said—*all* of it. Years back."

Now some hard eye has caught the clock and "Omigod, look, kids!" purses are snatched and snapped. "Toodles!"

Exit of many teachers to john, leaving Mrs. Eineman, who comes just a few minutes before school in the morning, examines her notices, and goes on to her room, where a quiet child has prepared her cup of tea. Mrs. Eineman has taught here several years, was a chemist, is married to a biochemist (though no one knows much else about her). Permissive methods, almost narrow about them. If a child throws a chair, she calmly asks why; if a teacher rebukes a child of hers in line for swearing, she may say, "Let him alone, he's disturbed." "But he said—" "Well, if he wants to talk that way, let him."

Every child in her room has a favorite painter whose work they study from great portfolios Mrs. Eineman provides. She gives special gifts for holidays: cactus for Easter, for Christmas a Japanese pencil with a bell. She is successful with children, in this school one of the most successful.

I get into 33B just at the bell. Feet thundering by outside. I get the window down from the top, place pile of notices and junk on desk, unlock back door—but don't make it up front in time. Kicks, sharp pounds—the door's falling open as I reach my desk. The first mass of Ricardo, Jesus, Marshall, Pablo, rolls in. Someone's playing handball with Roberto's book; he's trying to get it, a lot of screaming and yelling going on in the back.

The moment each seat is filled, we begin: salute to the flag, review of days of the week and months of the year. While I take attendance, they review sums in math notebooks. All present but Danny Aguilez. This is the norm in these schools: perfect attendance or else prolonged truancies; for we are the "highest-paid baby sitters."

Scrawls from home come next. "You quit make my kid cry, sign, M. Peraro." Some rather sad notes: "Pedro was out with asthma. The heat was off three days, we had to go to my sister's house." "Where's your note, José?" "My mama couldn't wri' it, she hadda washa baby." "Tell her I'll have to have it, or you must go to the office." He spent Friday on the subway as I know, for Carmen sidled up just after the bell and

11

told me, throwing a sexy little smirk to boys in the first row, "José wan' me come subways Friday, Miss Burke, he wan' do bad t'ings with me."

Door has slammed open with a pupil bringing a message, "Mr. Zang say, send down lesson plans." "Tell Mr. Zang I spent the week-end making alphabet picture cards. I haven't completed my plans." (This won't really take care of Zang, running the show below. But I write it out, the messenger waves to a few friends; he exits slamming.) On through the pile, to the clang and rattle of the room. Milk money, attendance percentage, book room, supply-room form, PTA notices, gym record, lunch cards, Red Cross, teachers' banquet, health folders. Confused welfare sheet on Pedro. "Pedro, your mama didn't fill this out." His head hangs. "Pedro, look at me! Will your mamma be at PTA?" (Of twenty-eight mothers, four have ever showed.) "Pedro's mama home inna Island again, Miss Burke," helpers supply, "he's living with his father and new mama, his old mama went away." "Wi' new *auntie*," Pedro finds his voice. "Well, your auntie will have to work this out with Mrs. Lawler—take this down to her. But be sure you come back. Wilfred, go with him."

The mere reverberation of the door unsettles them, and voices break forth. "Miss Burke, Danny Aguilez he been made a monitor!" "He cursed you, but Mr. Zang still gi' him a merit card, Miss Burke!" "They have to. Danny gets mad like he is now." "You fulla crap, man, Danny in sixt' gra' today." Children are getting out of their seats. *"Silence,* please! Everybody in their seats. *Not another word about Danny."* But I have to walk into the aisles beginning to fill with gum wrappers, scraps of paper. Nobody's done more than three or four problems ("I don't know these, I can' "). Some heads on desks. A few are staring moodily out at the rain. Miguel Rodriguez pulls at my skirt as I pass. "Miss Burke, my mama say tell you she wan' you to fill out those papers, them teet' t'ing I gotta—" "You'll have to come up to the desk, Miguel. . . . All right. For the what?" "For the Googy Clin'—" "For the Gug-gen-heim Clinic. Repeat it, Miguel: Gug-gen-heim." "Googy . . ."

By the time they're five, both the Negro and the Puerto Rican children tend to develop a certain arch little withdrawal smile: eyes down, lips pouting, cheek turned or nestled against shoulder. Sometimes it is fear or shyness; half the time it is handed down from older children. In any case the tiniest child does it: "Look at the person to whom you're talking, Miguel. Don't puff out your cheeks like that. Try again: Gug-gen-heim." "Goog—" We do this a few times. Then, because it's Monday or he's tired, Miguel does pronounce "Guggenheim" and "Clinic." Goes back to his seat, rather pleased with himself, to finish his sums.

But the trip to the desk has now stimulated the memory of Marshall R. "Miz' Burke, my mothah say why ain' I gettin milk like th' othahs?" "Because you're not in the lunch program." "She say tell you she wan' me gettin milk, tha's my ri'." "She didn't sign you up. She'll have to get the form from Mr. Hough. Now class, attention. It's nine-thirty. Let's stand, take a nice long stretch, before we correct our math—" (Crash. Messenger.) "Mr. Zang says you fill out dis supply form, and you send down dose healt' cards *dis* morning, and dese wit' 'em." (Crash. Slam.) The health cards have eaten up time for three weeks. Eyes have to be tested, each child weighed (send out and borrow the scale if you can get it), ears checked (takes half a morning; we sit out in the hall, a teacher with audiometer comes in). This with extra mimeo'd form from Mr. Spane, the school principal, on "Daily Health and Appearance Check" for teacher to fill out (how many without handkerchiefs, how many ears are dirty, etc.).

I'm occupied, so a fight starts. Three more minutes breaking this up, two to restore order, and monitors are just passing out phonics workbooks when Mr. Spane's morning voice suddenly fills the air above us. It is time for announcements. I have to go into the aisles—the children are talking and laughing freely now, and do so throughout Spane.

"Good morning, boys and girls! This is your old friend and principal, Mr. Spane. So sit tall and hearken, all!

(Pause.) "Well, Mr. Spane made a mistake, boys and girls. He left his glasses at home, and didn't see that the first message was for the teachers."

(Class is now thumbing noses and throwing fist-and-finger signs to the amplifier. "What's he talkin about?" "I can' hear him!" "I don' wanna hear him!")

"Come on then, teachers, sit tall! Mr. Pickard, I see you! Come 'way from that shelf of yummy cakes you're baking— Mr. Spane sees you! Sit tall, Miss Skally, Mrs. Eineman! You hard-working ladies are always trying to do two things at once! *I'm talking to every teacher in our school.*"

One notice escaped me; I was busy calming children in back, trying to keep their noise from bouncing off the amplifier back into his office. Another notice bubbled away, concerning "the Law . . . well-spring of Li-ber-ty. Hearken, teachers, because all supervisors and teachers will celebrate Law Day by appropriate classroom observances . . . to foster an abiding respect for law . . . moral strength. . . . Oh, just a minute. That's not until next month. *Law Day*, teachers— but all right, forget this *for the nonce,* teachers. Just

Mr. Spicer and Miss Bolby see me during the week on this —y'there, Spicer? And that's all, teachers, for the nonce.

(Pause. Sternly) "This is for the children. There will be no, repeat, *no* troubling of workmen, removal of materials, or any other destructive actions on the new housing project near our school. (Pause.) And now, children, here's our most important notice of the day! Sit tall!

"Well, boys and girls! Guess what Mr. Zang, Mr. Feil, and Mr. Spane have been up to for—oh, coupla *months* now, isn't it, Feil? Planning a surprise not only for the boys and girls at P.S. 200, but for our whole community! Do we all know what a Community is? Thinking caps on?

"Mr. Spane doesn't seem to hear any answers. Pickard? Don't you know what a Community is? I think we're letting Mr. Pickard get too tied down to that kitchen!

"A *Community* is our friends and neighbors, mommas and daddies, and *us*, all living and working and playing in the same place together. *Our.* Community is East Harlem, in the Borough of Manhattan, great city of New York!

"Now what should a community *be*? Why, full of life! Big things going on! Active! That's what we want our community to be! So Mr. Spane, Mr. Zang, and Mr. Feil have put their heads together, three thinking caps on, and set up an evening school. Now your mommas and daddies can come at night to the very same school where *you* have such fun every day! Yes! At night when *you're* home studying your lessons, Mommy and Daddy can sit at your little desks in school and learn many interesting things, just as you do, that can help them in their everyday lives. And this is where *you* come in!

"In each room, teachers distribute forms. Children take home—mind you, now—*home*. Not throw in streets and halls. Mommy and Daddy fill in at home and return. Got that, teachers? (Calling all teachers!) Children carry back to school, *tomorrow morning at the latest!* We all want East Harlem to be a live, active community! You want it, Mr. Pickard, Miss Skally, Mrs. Bergens: All our fine teachers want it! Last but not least, Mr. Zang, Mr. Feil, and Mr. Spane want it! Tomorrow morning at the latest!

"Good morning, boys and—no, wait a minute . . . where did I . . . one more short announcement here . . . (Pause. Crackling of paper.) Yes! Next week is going to be National Handkerchief Week, and the president for P.S. 200 will be . . . Mr. Zang.

"Good morning, boys and girls!"

By the time we've got Mr. Spane off the networks, it's 9:45. School has been in session for forty-five minutes. Phonics starts behind time, but as most children now know initial

14

and final consonants, a slight calm descends. The faster group is at work writing, the slower working orally with me. Then another messenger. (Crash.) Every shaky kid jumps up, drops what he's doing. "Heyyy, tha' Black Angel, he in sixt' gra'," they cry.

Reading, the dreary iron portals of ten o'clock, now overhangs the children. It's Monday too, the worst day, so violent and deadening are the week-ends in which these often malnourished and sick children have dribbled away hours of their strength on TV, movies, sitting on curbs. Some are now sucking thumbs, others peeping aloud or talking to themselves. But mostly they're just sitting and staring, mouths dropped open and left there. Heads stay in awkward positions. They are utterly exhausted. You'd think this would be a good day, but they are in a comatose state.

The slow group is promised, threatened or cajoled into taking out reading workbooks. To the other half, "Take out your readers." Groans and catcalls. At the word *reader,* Arturo, a disturbed child, calls, "Miss Bur', we go Release' Time today? We go Assemb'y today?"

Hands fly up before they know what page we're on. All will be eager to read. Few can read. Most are not bothered by the fact that they *can't* read.

Luce, who's found the right beginning page, is called on first today.[1] She is a pretty and intelligent child—stands up, rather pale this cold morning in a thin nylon dress. She wears pierced earrings like most of the little girls, a rain jacket all winter, has frequent asthma attacks, often is sniffling and sick-looking, but doesn't stay out of school. Luce takes a book home every night; privately, she has confided to me that she'd like to read well enough by the end of this semester to take home a book on nurses. "Here is Ted, here is Sally," she begins. Mutterings start at once. Hands in the air.

"You will not rudely interrupt Luce while she is reading." "Aw, *she* can' read." "You can' read neither." "Lemme read." "Mis' Burke, I don't know what page we' on." "I can' keep place, she read too fas'." "Someone stole my book, it's gone." A book is slammed shut. One kid gets up and walks out.

Luce wanders back: "Ted and Sally are going to—, to—" She looks up sadly. "Miss Burke, I read this in first grade."

"Yes, I know, dear, you've had this in your hands since first grade, but you've never learned to read it. If we had

---

[1] The Language Arts manual says there should be silent reading and denies the value of reading aloud for its own sake. But these bilingual children with their many special problems profit from frequent reading aloud.

more of some other easy book in the bookroom, we'd use them, but we don't. Let's go on. . . . If you don't know the word, is there a picture clue?" She plods ahead (through a thicket of whispers: "He cursed my mother." "This page is ripped out." "Can I go to the washroom?") because she's a sweet child; then falters, can't look at the words any longer. When her eyes lift, they contain the week-end: eight people in two rooms reeking with fried food, strangled at the end of four flights up. Babies, curses, TV mumbling, the people sitting as if drunk or dead, or else screaming shrill abuse. The stairs have trails of garbage, urine, even excrement.

Luce is now staring as in a trance, and she's permitted to sit down again this first hour. Edmund, who's been wildly waving, takes her place.

"Sally go."

"Sit down, Edmund. You're on the wrong page. Roberto." For two minutes Roberto reads beautifully, with such expression that the children listen.

"Now, who can tell what the story was about today? And how can it help us in our lives?" Hands wave, "I know, I know," and a satisfactory answer is given ("Be kind to your friends and share things"). "Good. Now we'll report on our library books. Manuel."

Manuel jumps up, dropping his book with a loud crash, on purpose. "Mis' Burke, Marshall cursed my mother." "Man, whut I say was . . ." A fight starts, kicking off noisy smaller fights across the room where children had been working quietly on their own, and for two minutes all work has to stop and "Heads down" until it's quiet.

"All right. The boys and girls who are writing may go back to their work. Marshall, tell about your book."

Thickset Marshall shoves something in his pocket, slides to his feet, giving his neighbor a kick on the way up. And stands grinning with no book.

"Sit down, Marshall. Israel."

Israel looks at the floor and scuffs his too-big shoes. "Where is your book, Israel? It's a library book. . . . Please see me after school today." Pablo, hero of Monday morning, has found his book, crosshatched with banana oil, but *there*. He pages through it, gradually recalls it's about a boy named Peter.

"Good. What does Peter do?"

"He go to a fireman house."

"Not a fireman's *own* house. What's the correct name of the place where Peter *visits* the fireman?"

"W'er fireman live."

"No, not where he lives but where he works, and its called a—"

He can't complete this and three other children who perused the book last week are called on before coherent recall of the twenty-page story, with bright red-and-gold illustrations above huge lettered lines on each page, is dragged out among them. Reading retardation is higher, it's true, than among children who lead richer lives outside of the schoolroom. And there are days of progress. But today? Miguel gives his report on a primer-level book named————. He reads: "Tony is . . . a . . ." Stops. He looks down. "I couldn' get past this word." The word is "happy"—he has had it for three years. "Well, how does Tony seem to feel, Miguel? Let's look at the picture—he is smiling, isn't he? When you're smiling you're—?"

Other children are calling out "happy" around him. He doesn't even hear. After a moment he answers, "I think . . . you go to a birthday party." Yet Miguel knows fifteen rock 'n' roll songs in Spanish with many verses, a dozen TV commercials word-perfect in English; can dance twenty versions of the Twist and Frug, can swim half a mile. His "language block" need not in itself be cited; in the Harlem Negro schools reading is just as low, children highly verbal, not bilingual.

Why can't he read? He is twelve years old. Some of many reasons are too much defeat; brings no experiences from home; lacks auditory discrimination (he can't hear the difference between *said* and *set*); no one speaks to him at home, or lets him finish a sentence or a thought. Finally, the *school* does not motivate him adequately to read. Teachers are often glad, and say so, when children in these schools stay home.

From good primary teachers at P.S. 200, I also know that four years ago Miguel and others who can't hear sounds in words this morning had a good foundation in phonics, lengthened their attention span, and showed signs of good intelligence for meaning. Since first grade then, they've stood still or regressed. But few teachers will admit it. *They* didn't fail. "They all finished the book this term—am I proud of 'em!" Skally: "Well, it's not been a complete waste this year. Half my fifth-graders are readin' at sixth-grade level." And the records—teachers' records—confirm it.

Miguel is still smiling, standing shaking his head, when the door opens and Mr. Zang moves in.

More or less together, all rise. "Good morning, Misser Zang."

"All right, all right kids, sit down. How many times I told you not to go through that routine when Mr. Zang comes in?

17

Mr. Zang cares more about *reading* progress than seeing you stand up like tall soldiers when he comes in." (To me, not too softly, "I've told you about that.") He's fishing for his notes. "This throws me *all* off." He is the deep-bottomed father of four, who provide him with frequent reference in making his points to my little group. ("Do you suppose Mr. Zang'd let his little Marcia come to school with a hanky as dirty as that? Of course not. And d'you know why not? . . . And I care for every one of you boys and girls just as much as I do for Marcia," etc.)

Lull in the room . . . mental current turned off the moment the door opened. Zang's now on a real fishing trip; children's eyes transfixed by his stomach. Miguel standing on one foot, talking to himself. Zang (digging): "Go right on with what you were doing, boys and girls. It looks mighty interesting."

"Who can tell Mr. Zang what we *were* doing?" Three hands move up.

Zang (whose notes have sprung from a pocket): "No, no, kids. That's okay. Mr. Zang always knows you're doing big stuff in this room. Now! Every eye on Mr. Zang! Every eye *right here*." (Two V-for-Victory fingers pushed between the eyebrows.) "Fingers out of our noses; let's save 'em to write with!

"Okay: did anyone hear someone say something *about* Mr. Zang over the P.A. this morning? C'mon, c'mon—where were *you* when Mr. Spane was telling about a swell surprise that's going to be unwrapped at P.S. 200 this week? Come on! Well, let's go back. What *is* the P.A.?"

Not a soul knows. None would know what was said on it if they *did* know. "The P.A.—the *amplifier*. We've got one in every single room in our school!" A hand creeps up. "There we go! Little girl."

"Miss Burke say my momma hafta come talk wit' her, but my momma couldn', she hadda go to Cleopatra."

"No, no. Not PTA, just *P.A.* Sit down, little girl. The P.A. is—no, good grief, I haven't got time for this. Here—the blanks—brief 'em before lunch, Miss Burke—Okay, gang! Next big thing! Sit up tall!

"The School Board. Who knows what the School Board is? —Put thinking caps on. Skoo-lll board.—That little boy. No, never mind. The School Board's the men and ladies who tell the children in all our New York schools what to do. Okay. School Board's told us spring's coming: go on more trips. Sure, they *want* boys and girls going places and seeing things. Somma the most *important* things boys and girls can learn about our city, y'won't *find* in any book! And we wantcha to learn everything you can, grow up proud and happy to be

18

living in the great East Harlem Community, Borough of Manhattan, City of New York! So that's what Mr. Zang's come to say this morning—green light, kids and Miss Burke, go on all the trips you want! And remember, make them happy, *learning* trips! Now Mr. Zang's gotta run along to the other rooms with the same good news. Good morning, boys and girls!" He's halfway to the door. I get to his side just in time to whisper, "No more trips this semester."

Trying to lunge out, he is impeded by Florence D., a Negro child who is withdrawn in the pattern of deepest Harlem. She's huddled in her blue coat outside the door—hasn't had the coat off all year.

Zang's eyes and mine meet, bringing back the Thursday scene of that first-floor corridor, and Zang, and three other assistant principals having a laugh over their bowling scores. Danny spitting, fighting, cursing; what Zang said was, "Yes *indeed*. I'll talk to this young man *in my office.*" Dragged Danny off (Danny getting in a bite on the wrist), threw him into the office, and locked the door. Came back to his audience of five adults, looking around for Bill, the janitor. I said, "But what are we going to do about him?" "Oh, don't worry about *that*. Can't have things like *that* going on. I'll advise you— tomorrow at the latest. Hey—Bill!"

I mention the incident to Mr. Zang again this morning, one week later.

"Oh yeah, Aguilez, quite an acting-out kid all right. Listen, I've had some thoughts on that. They haven't quite jelled yet. Listen, there're some forms—I'll send up—now I've just *got* to—"

"Mr. Zang, what's going to happen to Danny? (Back there —stop the fooling back there.) Pablo, quickly tell Mr. Zang what your book was about."

"It about—"

"Good; good boy. Evening school: brief the kids. You got a fine teacher here, kids, who loves you very much. Take care of her." Slam. Slam back open long enough for his arm to thrust in Florence D., and he's gone.

DANNY AGUILEZ

He is a stocky, low-slung boy, made of steel, agile; he has great dark eyes that he does so many things with, a masculine brow. He was born in the United States—on his mother's side is the third welfare generation. At a prekindergarten age he attacked his sister with a broken bottle, and his

19

aunt (his mother was then back in Puerto Rico) called the police. He was committed to Bellevue. A week later the father returned and rushed down to remove him—he's not been under observation since that time. Besides a half-brother and half-sister in Puerto Rico, Danny has a school-age brother, a sister who is kept home much of the term as a baby sitter, a baby brother and a baby sister. All are on welfare, except the aunt who works in a bead factory and helps out when she can with a few dollars a month.

Having saved Danny from Bellevue, the father beat him up a few times—once with tire chains—and disappeared. He is now being sought by the Social Welfare Department—but at this point we may ask the City and the State: What has become of Danny, whose short years have been spent not in a family but among public officers—case workers, police, truant officers, psychiatrists, teachers?

Except for a Brooklyn period, when a teacher was dismissed for striking him, he's been in P.S. 200 for years. Conservatively, there are many hundreds like him in the schools today.[2] True, it is often best in theory, other things being equal, for a disturbed child to be in a normal school environment. But did this happen with Danny—did being in P.S. 200 help him or make him sicker? For two years, Skally taught in Harlem, where rocks and knives, child molestation were frequent occurrences. A murder was committed within the school's walls. But the lethal elements in that school were growing up by a kind of terrible norm, "early habitual delinquents" of a totally sick milieu. The two environments are not comparable. With a boy such as Danny the school had more chance. Suppose it had set up, as it did not, a real psychiatric program linked with a crash drive on reading in first and second grades. (Think of the tremendous ego-building power of learning to read.) The school might act as the threshold of recovery for any sick child. Now, it is too late to know what might have happened with Danny if the school at an early date had done these things for him. It didn't, and he arrived in fourth grade strongly antisocial, non-reading, schizoid,[3] talking to himself. Any threat to his security—he loses a monitor's job; an aide

[2] That is to say, identified as "disturbed." The Community Health Board in 1960 estimaed that 10 to 20 per cent of the 978,000 children then in school actually needed psychiatric help. About 36,000 actually receive some form of mental health service each year. (N.Y.C. Community Council figures)

[3] P.S. 200 psychiatric file. Julius Horowitz, consultant on social welfare to the N.Y. State Senate majority leader, has written that "the welfare slums . . . breed schizophrenia in children faster than the slums of the nineteenth century bred tuberculosis."

suggests he may not roam the halls—and he bursts into screams. He hears voices threatening to kill him on TV. He runs out of classrooms, out of the building. He screams at teachers.

This year, for the first time in four years, he's been put on psychiatric referral. Immediately after that, a curtain of silence fell around him and all that concerned him. He's defunct, a case being disposed of. Only two of the many teachers who had direct contact with Danny will ask even a casual question aloud about him (though everyone does say, "Really sick kid. Breaks your heart."). Why? The three years up to now must be laid to rest. Five career administrators, all high-salaried, two of them still qualifying, wish to be known as tough and competent with the Board. None of them in three years ever took a straight forty-five minutes with this boy. The louder he screams now, the quieter it grows around him. Soon another city agency will pick up the burden; meanwhile, no talking about Danny, no raising questions. It was nobody's fault. And no classroom teacher, up to this year, has written anything on Danny's record about aberrant behavior.

How did he get by four years? His second- and third-grade teachers did often send him down to Guidance. Notes came back: "Needs praise and recognition—made to feel 'ten feet tall.'" Also, for all the turmoil, P.S. 200 is a dead backwater in which anything can go on indefinitely before a principal steps out of an office. Three days ago, Mrs. Eineman noticed that a degenerate had wandered into the building and was exposing himself outside her room. Two days in a row she called down for a corridor guard. No guard came, but Feil called up later to say, "I want a complete written report on this immediately."

All the administration wants for Danny now are rooms to shock-absorb him until he's off its hands. Of the rooms on my floor (there are ten third- and fourth-grade level) that could serve as receptacles for Danny since September, several are chaotic. One of these is "creative"—all gaily painted skyscrapers made of shoe boxes, shrubbery planted with identifying colored leaves; mobiles; children working on projects of rice paddies and dikes; but also dirty and full of screaming. A second room has a male teacher, himself fastidious in dress but lazy, withdrawn from the children. The windows are closed in this room, the air is noisome and stifling; crayons and shrieks fly through it: "I wanna yellow, I wanna yellow."

Of several quiet rooms, some are like mine, with five or six disturbed children each, but relatively controlled. Danny had been in most of the good rooms—he tore them apart.

21

The bad ones can't contain him. They get the breaks. I hadn't had him, and my turn came.

At that time the children were making some headway reading. Mrs. Abernathy and Mr. Yount were still taking retarded readers out of the room. It was a classroom just beginning to function. Then Danny was put inside.

Soon the room was revolving around the new violent center: his cries—usually in Spanish—"I won't! I won't!" his tearing up of books, pulling hair, punching children if they had something he wanted, running into corners head first. Work would now be brought to a dead halt many times a day, the children's psychic energy drained, while Danny resolved conflicts.

Above all, any control of himself slipped farther out of his power each day. Last year it took Mrs. Eineman and Miss Campbell together, scratching and puffing, to drag him down a flight of stairs. He was smaller, the teachers were stronger; now he's stronger. He can take on every boy in the room. Two or three boys would try to pull him off a child; he could overturn both of them.—Even stranger, the borderline nature of it all. Sometimes the rage would suddenly subside; he'd sit down and ask the child next to him, "What page we on?" Exhausted after an outburst, hoping you'd be his friend again, he'd come up and quietly sing a song just for you. A third-grade teacher told me how, for a week at a time, he'd illustrate his new vocabulary words in color, though even then, she said, the plateau periods were growing shorter. By the time I got him, Danny could no longer be contained in any room. Children were drawn into his reflexes—each day new deeper waves of nervous sighs passing through them, and in his most desperate moments he'd attack me. On his last high-rage afternoon he swung a chair at my head. I kept hands off him, but Zang knew I wasn't safe any more with him and removed the boy. In a few days the room came back to normal.

Danny was sent on to Mrs. Eineman, whose room is also "tightly structured" (disciplined), where he threw a chair at a child. Someone had erased the board when it was his job. On to strong Mr. Dion, then to Mr. Pickard of the 70-80 I.Q.'s fourth, to see if the lower mental key would work. Mr. Pickard is very gentle, but once I met him in the hall slamming Danny against the wall. Nothing had worked by Christmas. A rerun in Mr. Dion's room, where he broke ten recorders.

I came back from Christmas to find him re-registered in my class. I sent him down to Mr. Zang—a guard brought him back, with some forms and a note that Zang was out. I put the class on alphabetizing and filled out the forms. Danny had thrown himself into a corner, where he sobbed and screamed.

I couldn't reach Guidance, and sent the forms down to the psychiatric social worker, who called me back in an hour: "What prompted the incident? This is not a complete anecdotal record. Please reconstruct the incident." I said, "The incident is going on now—that's him you hear screaming." "Well, we need an anecdotal record," she told me and hung up.

At 2:45 I put the room in charge of an aide and went out to get anyone I could before 3:00 P.M., which Mr. Dion calls "Track Hour." ("Everyone's trying out for the 1968 Olympics.") As I approached the office, Assistant Principal Spicer was just slipping out to go to his night job. He is a neat, nervous, shifty person. His fingers curve over a polished attaché case. He was yards down the hall before I could catch up with him. I was shaking.

He tried to talk me down till we got to the stairs, then decided he'd have to "deal with the problem"—the problem of me bothering him, that is. It was nearing three o'clock.

Spicer's number two chin was trembling. His eye tried to snag each passing scurrier. "Look here, Miss Burke. How about a real talk on this thing in my office on Wednesday?"

"No, I don't want a real talk; just not to see Danny tomorrow morning in class." "Look, everyone's having a turn at this kid—" and Spicer's voice moved on far away, about diagnostic work-ups, processing, these things take time, and "We'll have him in a 600 School [for "problems"] by end of term. Oh, hey there, Griff," he called, trying to walk around me, "you get those charts done for statistics class—? Look, Miss Burke, we've got to talk on this later."

"Mr. Spicer, Danny has been here for four years. He is a sick and such a miserably unhappy child. It's not his fault. But I can't help him—can't we get him to those who will? He should have been referred a year ago—an outpatient clinic —there were many incidents last year. He could have been screened by now. But never mind. All I want—now—is him out of my class. He's stealing time away from other little children who are working against odds; he's getting all my time. And still getting sicker . . ."

To this Spicer answered, "If you think *he's* crazy, you should see his brother in sixth grade."

Long pause. An aide carrying some interracial puppets marched past, saying, "Now we're going to tell a story through charades," to three disruptive children who were punching each other and squashing bubble gum in each other's jaws; followed by Betty Zetter, who publishes papers on reading improvement and is on hundreds of block committees, trotting to keep up with them, saying, "Well that's not nice, to run like that."

"Miss Burke. We've got a lot of things cooking—"

"Amy Katz told me the child was in four classes last year, Mr. Spicer. Aguilez tattooed his arm with a pin and India ink this morning. He stuck scissors into the child across from him—she wouldn't give him a crayon."

"Miss Burke, I'll send up some B.C.G. forms; sure, we'll try to expedite it, but you know the forms. I'll send up forms. You fill them, you'll feel better."

"I filled out the B.C.G. forms, I spent last week-end on other forms. And you know it."

"Miss Burke, we're doing our best. You got him back because you didn't strike him. You have a tightly structured room. The family's just waiting. They'll press charges at the drop of a hat. They've collected three thousand dollars from the City already. The kid's dynamite. Oh—*five after three!*" moaned Spicer. "Miss Burke, I'll tell you. He's on every waiting list in the city. The Youth Board's trying, but the guys down there tell me he's a creampuff compared to what they have pending. We *have* to wait. Pull-llleease . . . be reasonable. Every teacher has five or six nuts. Miss Skally make take him —Yes. I think that's in the offing."

I said, "I'm not accountable for him tomorrow."

But Danny stayed until the day in the corridor with Zang, when I told Zang I might resign, and Danny was taken away.

He was then dropped in and out of some more rooms. Joe Dion shared my curiosity about what would happen to Danny. But he laughed at my folly, to think the forms I wrote out on a week-end would serve any purpose. "They'll park him with Skally awhile—she runs a smooth room," said Joe, meaning her tendency to let disrupters out of the room. The police picked up one such kid this month over on the other side of Central Park—she'd let him out. He was trouble in class; she never worried about the truancy. "But forms—don't be naïve, comrade. I used to write-up and follow-up too. Long ago. You miss the point—the forms are to keep you busy and out of the whole thing, not in it. Your form may wind all the way down to City Hall, it won't affect the poor kid. And, you may still get him back."

Thursday afternoon came—dead day. Half the room, lucky ones, had gone whooping off to Released Time. Down on the street I could hear the priests saying, "Get in line. Cut that out. Get in line." At 2:30, Mr. Dion poked his head in with two kids who were hitting each other with their *Numbers Are Fun* books. "These're all I got left in my stocking—they're going down to color," said Mr. Dion happily. But the fifteen

24

children in my room were reading, not badly. It was pointless to keep stuffing this story down them about Dick and Jane coming over to play, bringing some cat or squirrel along to play with Ted and Sally's dog; children and animals having a ball around a tree in an elm-decked suburb. I said we'd finish three pages and close books, then I'd read *Peter Pan* to them until three. Happily the children tackled the three pages. When the room was quiet I began: "One night, as Wendy lay dreaming in her bed—"

Shriek from a little girl. Danny Aguilez had crept in the door and faced us, clutching a math compass, the long piercing stick end forward, grinning. We'd almost forgotten him! Children began standing up, whimpering—one boy, Ephraim, was muttering in Spanish. Ephraim must have been the target. I never got the whole story—a fight over a basketball at noon, so Danny had come back to mete out justice to former class-mates.

Whispering "Don' you come ne' me," in my direction, he circled fast backward across the room, flourishing the weapon, imitating his hero, the Viceroys' leader. I knew it was Zang's day to go to night class. I dared not pick up the phone. Jesus on the outside row was signaled to slip down to the office.

Danny reached the window and jumped up on the sill with a yell. He stalked up and down the sill, panting and yelling, then spitting out, "I'm gonna t'row, Ephraim. Ephraim, you gettin dis!" The room was immobile. He switched to Spanish as voices rose rapidly, then soared to screams. Between screams the room was dead silent; you could hear the clock.

Steps outside. Jesus the messenger appeared panting in the doorway. He drew a breath before picking up his neat, tapered little steps to come up and stand before me—I couldn't move—straight-faced and simple, and deliver the message he'd been given: "You tell Miss Burke that's her tough luck."

The bell rang. Three classes began to pass outside the room. Inside, Danny went berserk. He grabbed the window pole, drove it through the bottom pane, screaming as glass showered. The trampling in the corridor drowned his screams. He leaped down onto desks under the window, his head jerking. He slammed down chairs. Sixth grade was now crashing past, a molten cascade of teen-agers—not a face turning toward us, the door open on the frozen scene and screaming boy. Yelling, writhing, they poured past, waving torsos, bee-hive hairdos and movie magazines at each other, while their custodian, Miss Beale, (who next day said she'd noticed nothing out of order) paced thoughtfully beside.

The corridor emptied fast; he went on screaming. It was many minutes before Spicer appeared, little blue eyes and freckled lids screwed up with hate, Bill the guard beside him, to see why 33B wasn't dismissed. Danny had jumped back up on the ledge and stood screaming. As Bill moved in, he hit a blood-curdling scream and fell to his knees, stabbing at the children below him. He missed Ephraim . . . slid off the ledge onto piles of broken glass. Bill flew across the room and pinned the boy down on the floor.

This wasn't quite the end. Just after three the next day, the door opened and Danny's small, frightened mother stood outside. Once before I'd met her, having gone to Danny's home when he'd run away for two days. She tried not to cry that day, and, except for saying over and over, "I don't want no trouble," and once the phrase of Puerto Rican women, "You're his mother in the school," could not communicate. She was a soft-voiced woman, as sick and as bewildered as Danny, who had at one time been beautiful. She kept her purse on her shoulder, but no one was there in the basement apartment with no furniture. Today, a small boy friend of Danny's was at her side. He had helped her find the room, and now began translating at once for her:

"Where is he, he ran out of the room, where is he? What did he do? . . . I don't want no trouble. I want him in the room, I want him to be a good boy." She was crying. "I don't want all this trouble, this trouble."

———————

It is now nearly 10:30 and no Mrs. Abernathy. I put the faster group on reading workbooks, her slower group on their assignment. Mrs. Abernathy is Corrective Reading Teacher. Mr. Yount is Reading Improvement Teacher. Both were very helpful for some time. Then Mr. Yount dropped off (he's been hiding out, studying for assistant-principal exams in his office most of the school day), and Mrs. Abernathy began coming late.

Mrs. Abernathy is conscientious, brings special teaching aids to her work, and knows the teaching of reading, but has become very uneasy toward the children since she began coming late. She has been in P.S. 200 for several years. She's hit the circle that awaits the sensitive teacher—can't take any more, will quit if she isn't let out of the classroom. She becomes a specialist or supervisor. A less competent teacher takes her place. My slower reading group is scheduled for 33J, a big classroom. Mrs. Abernathy is supposed to take them out of the room. But lately, her friends Miss Perez, Mrs. Rumstedt, Mr. Kaplan have taken to holding "curriculum meetings" (which develop into coffee and cigarette breaks) in 33J.

There is not much I can do. Mr. Zang drives Mrs. Abernathy to school in the mornings. She's also grown very critical. Amy Katz said, "She's been getting in on that coffeepot in 33J, that's all. That's why she's been so critical lately."

Amy found some fifth grade social science books in the basement this month—beautiful covers and illustrations, stacked to the ceiling, have never been opened. Sixth, seventh, even eighth grade will never read well enough to read them. Amy took them up to her fifth grade for her faster readers— they're at third-grade level but progressing rapidly. The maps and noble engravings would inspire any class with the excitement, the pleasure, of learning.

When Mrs. Abernathy's eye fell on the new treasure, she told Amy simply, *"These books are threatening, Miss Katz."* And back they went to the basement where, said Amy who accompanied them down, six A.D.N.S. (All Day Neighborhood Schools) teachers were busy unpacking more crates of new books, and next door to the book room the second grade was doing Dutch dances. (They do a lot of dancing in second grade, and when the lunchroom's occupied by third grade doing square dances, second grade does its dancing next to the book room.) That same week I'd picked up second-hand copies of *National Geographic, Natural History,* and other magazines for our library shelf. "You're not being fair to them," said Mrs. Abernathy. "You must not make these demands. Stick to the books they can read."

"But I often read to the children from them. We talk about all the birds—see these fine color photographs of the swamp birds, scavengers, birds of prey. It's a reward for finishing work pages. The children's interest is so strong—you should see them struggling to read these magazines! Last week Carlos almost cried because he couldn't read the caption under a picture of a snowy egret."

"That's what I mean. You're not being fair."

"But then he went to work—he took the magazine home. Thursday he could read, 'This is a snowy egret.' "

"And will that help him in the reader? You're arousing desire in him for something he can't achieve. We try to treat the child as a decent human being," she concluded—as so often.

She's also been made Cultural Coordinator between "Higher Horizons" and the Reading Program. This week a sudden burgeoning—Abernathy's work—of posters and reading displays on first-floor walls. Some Puerto Rican area supervisors were due on a flying visit (though few of us will get to see

...—they only go to the brightest classes). Friday she hurried into my room to get material for a display. "I want everything your room's been doing for Choral Speaking," said Abernathy. "Now how about those lovely big illustrations you had in Assembly last week for *Winnie-the-Pooh?*" I didn't really want to take time out helping Mrs. Abernathy deck up halls for supervisors. One group was reading; another group was on phonics workbooks. How about later? But Abernathy had now noticed "March 21" in cursive writing on the board, a sight which always seems to make her half lose her mind. She kept hold of herself this morning, just murmured, staring, "Oh . . . I'll wait. Please go right on with what you're doing. As you know, Miss Burke, you're not to teach them handwriting until they're reading on second-grade level. It's too confusing to a child."

"Mrs. Abernathy, many examiners have proved cursive is easier to learn than printing. In the Montessori and other methods, the children never learn to print."

"They simply can't do it, Miss Burke."

"Boys and girls, hold up this morning's class papers—they are doing it, Mrs. Abernathy. They're eleven years old."

But she wouldn't look at the papers. And even though her group is reading aloud because she is late, I expect trouble this morning.

It's still some minutes before we hear her calling from the door, "Good morning, children! Are we ready to take a trip?" Books slam shut—no trouble there—as she continues, gliding briskly to the back of the room, "Yes, we're 'going to the country' with Ted and Sally, where we'll see many wonderful things we can't in the city! And someone else is going today, I believe—Ted and Sally's puppy, who'll meet a friendly new animal in the country! Are we ready for the fun? All aboard! . . . Now, who'll bring Mrs. Abernathy her chair?" Big haul of chairs on all fours, rearward—new diversion, which gets everyone excited. "Don' you touch my a'm, man, I warnin you." "Don't curse my mother!" "I'm bringing the chair; you brought it yesterday."

"We're on a *train* now, boys and girls! Let's lock our lips and throw the key away out the window!" Mrs. Abernathy calls, putting up primer charts "The Puppy and the Rabbit" for these eleven-year-olds, most of whom were born in the United States and started kindergarten at five years.

The hubbub begins: emotionally shaky children who can't read doing phonics in front, even shakier but slower children being told in back, "Let's open to the picture of the train getting itself all ready to leave its home, the station. It's taking Ted and Sally and Tuffy *to the country!* It's a *happy*

28

rain. How can we tell? . . . well, just look at the big smile
's wearing on its engine! Who knows what the engine does?"

"Miz' Abby, we awready had dis story today."

"Mrs. Ab-er-nathy, Marshall."

"Mis' Abio, we had about that puppy-rabbit ina country
oday."

"No, no, Miguel, you're thinking of another puppy we had
such fun with last month. That was another book. Who can
ell the name of the reader we're reading now?" The fifteen
children in front are now stirring, giggling, and twisting,
crying to fishhook their friends' eyes out of the slow group
n back. Abernathy's rimless glasses seem to rotate slowly
before fixing themselves on me.

"You've been through the story, Miss Burke?"

"Well, we went as far as—"

"You've conducted them far enough that initial expectation
can no longer be aroused?"

"Mrs. Abernathy, there *is* no—yes . . . we have been
through it."

"Well, children . . . we'll just have to start over again.
Could you give me the page number, Miss Burke?"

Meanwhile they've found the initial-expectation page all
right. Resistance is shaping in a solid, muttering child wall.
"*I* ain' readin dis story again." "I ain' *nevah* goin look at it
again." "I hate Ted, I hate ol' Sally more. Who cares about
that ol' red wagon and kitten they drag aroun' in it." "I rea'
it today, and I rea' it in firs' gra'."

Fifteen minutes later, front: we're adding *ing* to root words.
"If Ted rides, Roderigo, he is—?" "Riding." "Good. Call on
another child, Roderigo." Rear: "*Frame* the word. Finger on
each side. Now what do you see? What do you see?—Just a
moment. Are you on the right page, Carmacita?" The room is
suppressed uproar. Abernathy is wearing a smile like a tied-
on bandage. No trouble about the noise, though. Noise doesn't
exist. Interruptions permissively treated. "Marshall, what do
you see?" "Mis' Abernath', Marshall took my pencil." "I *ain'*
took, he *trade* for his yo-yo wi' me, Miz Abby." (Handbook:
"We must give scope and understanding to that intense and
growing *êthique* of the fourth-grader.") At times the back of
the room seems to have swung around entirely with a big clatter
of chairs, clockwise. To add to everything else, the hall door's
been left open. Abernathy's girl friend, Svenson, and another
teacher outside: "Yes . . . Ninety-first Street outlet . . . I hear
they have some pretty good stuff there."

"Bianca, please close the door."

But Mrs. Abernathy rises, carrying today's glacial smile upward, and glides. "*Please,* Miss Burke." All the slow-group

books bang shut behind her. Svenson leans in as her boss approaches. "So you need anything else, Mrs. Abernathy?"

"No, Mrs. Svenson, we're all aboard for the country—our train's just a little late pulling out. —No, I'll see you later about that whole problem. Thank you for waiting."

Teacher: "Workbooks, Mrs. Abernathy? We've needed them for a week."

Dirty look from Svenson, who lists it, however, and sends down Pablo with a note. Svenson-teacher conversation resumes outside. Carlos returns with the wrong workbooks.

"All right. We'll start with these, boys and girls. They're one grade behind us so they should be really easy. Monitors, see if you can pass these out quietly."

"We can' do this kin' work," they say immediately. "These too hard for us." "I ain' gonna work this workbook."

"No, these aren't the *right* workbooks, boys and girls, but let's use them as a little review. Let's settle down and be happy."

Mrs. Abernathy's hearing has suddenly returned to her. Long, gray raised eyebrows from the back. "Really, Miss Burke, they read *very* well. Beautiful reading experience in here one day last week—let me see—Wednesday! Let's not forget to praise them when it's due, Miss Burke."

"Mrs. Abernathy, these children have not really learned to read."

"They've been *well* taught, Miss Burke. All our teachers are doing their best."

"Their files said 3.1 when I started, you mean? Then why didn't they know *a, e, i ,o,* and *u?*"

All the children are now out of their seats and talking; I've let my temper slip and it's too late. But Mrs. Abernathy arm-gathers materials and glides in perfect calm to the door. "Mrs. Abernathy, there *is* a certain resistance to learning here," I say to her through the din.

"We have one or two children that don't apply themselves, but really it's a beautiful class," she firmly answers. "I'll be back on Friday, boys and girls, to hear about the library books. But Roberto, let's remember, dear, to ask the librarian if she has some other kind of story than Bible books. The story of Moses finding the baby was very colorful and exciting, but we come from many different religious backgrounds. Let's find stories we can all share."

To me: "They're underprivileged but teachable, Miss Burke. We're here for the children and for no other reason."

Miss Moyle, an O.P.T. teacher (supplementary teachers who relieve the regular classroom teacher), comes in at 11:00 for

ocial studies. These children are scheduled to study (the syl-
labus says they *do* study) math, social studies, science, music,
and art, although they can't read. Miss Moyle is very amiable
with teachers, recently engaged, salt-and-pepper gray in her
hair, and happy.

For a month we had walk-ups and skyscrapers, multiple
dwellings, and the subway. "You'd be amazed," Moyle would
insist, "how many of the children just don't know what the
subway is."

"But Miss Moyle, all the children go to every borough
with their families over the week-end, visiting relatives, staying overnight. The little boys sneak on and ride the subway
all day Saturday by themselves. They ride all over New
York; they go to Coney Island, to Forty-second Street,
and get themselves home on the subways."

Moyle: "Many of them have simply never seen a subway.
Many of these children, dwelling in the world's largest
metropolitan area, simply grow up without having learned
what 'sub-way' means. We're here to teach them about their
cultural environment, such as the subway."

February was Manhattan Island. "We're going to learn
many wonderful things about Manhattan Island." "They
don't know their street addresses," objected Miss Peruzzi
when Moyle first hit 3B. "None of them know their birth-
days; a few can't spell their names."

"Now put everything away and sit tall. How many children
know what the Atlantic Ocean is?—Put that away.—Today
we're going to play a game to learn many wonderful
things about the Atlantic Ocean. Let's say that together,
children . . . that's right . . . once again, rounding our lips
when we say 'O-cean'—good! fine!—and about Manhattan
Island on which we live. Manhattan Island is in the Atlantic
Ocean. Now who knows what an eye-land is?" (Eyes not
exactly where she wants them but wandering from sparkler,
to dapper suited front, to graying hair.)

"Now some of us are going to come up front—no, no,
not until Miss Moyle calls on just four *quiet* children who
don't leave seats until she says—and join hands.

"Put that away. I want your eyes looking at *me*.

"All right: you, you, you, my dear, and you. Now a fifth
child. That child is to have a very important part in our
play. *We're going to make our own Manhattan Island.* I'm
going to look for the very tallest and ready-est . . . Edwin!
Very well, Edwin, you may come up front too. (Put that
away. I don't want to speak to you again.) Edwin is going
to be Manhattan Island.

"—I'm going to send you—this girl—back to your seat

31

if you can't play your part gently. Edwin, haven't you got a hanky, dear? You should use a hanky for that.

"Again, mouse steps back and forth! Now what is it we're looking at, children in seats? What are Edwin and the four children pouring back and forth on him, showing us?"

Silence. Deep contemplation. Four answers are garnered from the room:

"Hol' hans'."

"Play house?"

"———" (in Spanish, which "elicits" big, general dirty laugh).

"Ring-aroun'-a-rosy."

Last month, one solid month, was the Community. ". . . The Community is made up of many wonderful workers. Can anyone name a worker? No one? Surely someone knows the name of *one* kind of worker. Good, I knew you did! All right, that little boy."

"Policeman."

"Good. What does the policeman do?"

"He'p us."

"Good! *Fine! How* does he help us?"

"He our fren'."

"Yes, good, but *how* is he our friend? *How* does he help us?"

Lots of trouble on this one. Much time consumed. Finally, something like "he'p a los' chil' fin' he way home," is "elicited."

"Good! *Very* good! Now let's think of some other kinds of workers. Who can name another kind of wonderful worker?"

"Policeman," answer several together.

"Yes, but still another kind! We'd have a funny kind of Community, wouldn't we, if we were *all* policemen?" Frowns, sulks, drop toward apathy again.

"Let's put on our thinking caps. *All* the kinds of wonderful workers we know. What about people who help us learn many wonderful things? What kind of workers are they?" Silence . . . *"There* goes a hand up. All right, little boy with the bandage. Can't you ask Mommy to change that bandage, dear? All right."

"Teach'."

"Good! And what good workers they are, too, your wonderful teacher here, and me, and Mr. Zang and Mrs. Abernathy—how really *hard* we work, don't we?"

Fireman, Nurse, even Jim the Friendly Street Cleaner, each in turn is elicited. Then on to a cloudier side of the subject. "What about *our own parents*, who work so hard to care for us? What kind of work do *they* do?" Many children really don't know what she's talking about. A few have fallen to dreaming again. "Well, what about *our fathers?* Don't our fathers work so *very* hard, coming home at the end of day all tired but happy, too, because they've been working to earn money for our food and clothes?" This reminds them of lunch. "Good! *I* see a hand that knows the answer!" "Miss Moily, w'en bell time?"

"Quite soon, dear. Now everyone *think*. Thinking caps on tight, pulled *way* down for a cold, cold day, down to our *ears. What kind of work do our fathers do?*" Not six fathers in the room have jobs, as Miss Moyle might know if she kept her eyes open coming along ——th Street in the morning. But on she goes, question, hint, probe. Finally lets it drop, provisionally.

"But *someone* in our family works, or we wouldn't *be* here with our food and clothes, would we, we wouldn't have *any*thing! Who in our family works?" Mommy. "But then, what does Mommy do, all day, what *kind* of work, when she goes away and doesn't come home until sunset time?" Three minutes produce two mommies who work in the garment district, one who works stringing jewelry. "Fine! *Very* good! How interesting and wonderful a talk we've had this morning, boys and girls. And now it's time for l——
. . . for Miss Moyle to go.

"But first, Miss Moyle wants each child to do something for her. Each child is to go home and search in the newspaper tonight for a picture of a wonderful worker. Someone in our big wonderful city on Manhattan Island, who's doing some kind of work. For example: a picture of a worker in the *garment district* working: how wonderfully and carefully she's pulling her needle in and out of the cloth that will turn into trousers for a little boy or skirt for a little girl. Take notebook paper; use one side only; paste neatly just at each corner. And one more thing. How many think the can write a nice sentence, telling what the worker in the picture is working at?" (No child in this room could write a full sentence. But every hand flies up.) "Good, *good!* I knew that's what you'd like to do for Miss Moyle. And she'll be back tomorrow at eleven o'clock"—heading for the door— "to see how intelligent you are. I know we're going to have some won—"

"Mis' Zangy?"

"I'm Miss Moyle, dear."

"We don' have no newspaper." She has to return and wring this out. Magazines? No, no magazines. But surely

33

a Spanish-language newspaper? That would be perfectly fine for a worker picture. No, no Spanish. "But then your next-door neigh-bor must have a newspaper he or she would gladly give you for your picture." Ignores the silence. (Some aren't sure what a neighbor is.) "Fine. How many are going to have the assignment tomorrow? Won-derful! Good morning, boys and girls."

Of today, third session on New York State, I will just say that Miss Moyle could not believe they didn't remember one fact from last week. Angel at last refused to answer. He laid his head down on his desk and went to sleep. It's because they're not interested. Angel is simply not interested —yet. "Our job is to help him be interested," says Miss Moyle. "He'll enter into situations creatively when they involve him. Learning's got to be fun."

When she'd gone, I woke Angel and we had a talk. I outlined to him his present and future in the class. He did get back his memory. And we found he was able to repeat back a dozen facts: New York State is bounded on the east by the Atlantic; the governor lives in Albany; Henry Hudson was an explorer; New York was called New Amsterdam, and so on. And this with messages winging between: Youth and Adult Center forms; Dental Control Sheet; check periodically that children are under treatment, completion date, etc.; cumulative records or transfer slips: "Be sure to enter grades in Academic Progress as well as in Personality Growth"; PTA forms; something from Mayor Wagner about registering to vote; and always the pleas or whinings: "Are we goin gym today?" "Miss Burke, when's Rumpelstilts?" and Angel sobbing in between facts, "My mudder'll get you in court for dis."

Teachers' lunchroom is empty today but for Miss Peruzzi, who goes around with liberal Catholic groups, young couples who meet Friday nights in each other's apartments and wish to help the poor. And some of them do: her friends, Gerald and Susan, who drive her with her children to the country on Saturdays—people who never did things like that before. Others get lost in theory. Peruzzi is the quietest teacher in school, always thinking of what Saint Francis of Assisi wrote long ago about the poor or what Mr. Ephraimson, her supervisor, said yesterday on the same subject; or kissing her charges, trying to make up for all the ills of society. However, she's honest about where she stands ("Oh, I have a long way to go. . . . I wish the supervisor would spend more time in my room.") and a good teacher with her retarded children, who leave her in June still thinking life is magic, worth learning to read for. She also had Danny Aguilez (he kicked her in the stomach) in between Mr. Dion and Mr. Pickard, and Danny's poor mother on a bad day. Danny hung on the trembling mother's skirts, yelling "Gimme a quarter" in English and Spanish; then a policeman came in off the beat —all this in Peruzzi's room, during a class—looking for Danny. "My mind just went blank," says Peruzzi. "And I— I was trying to pray for all of them; but the words just wouldn't come."

She has the latest thing from the grapevine this noon. "Oh, Danny's not getting *out*. I don't know why Mr. Spicer implied that. In spite of that scene in your room—oh, everyone's heard about that! What was it? Was he trying to kill children? Really, you'd think that *now* they'd—but no, Danny's staying. Skally's going to take him. She made a deal with the office—she gets to teach that top sixth next year, she takes Danny now."

I take a sip of coffee, then it occurs to me, "Skally's quite good but she'll only teach bright children, not retarded in any way. Danny's a bit emotionally retarded, wouldn't you say? She tried to trade a kid in her room with me for Roderigo when I first came here—she'd give me Israel as a throw-in. Roderigo is an artist. She shops around for a nice room. But wait a minute, what's wrong with the way Al's teaching top sixth now—what are they doing with Al?"

"Well, I suppose they'll do something else with Al," says Miss Peruzzi, who doesn't like to go into things too deeply. "I guess they think if she keeps Danny more than six weeks she *should* get a top class, sort of a strength prize."

"And he is going to sit here another semester, getting sicker?"

"Well, Skally will probably leave him out in the hall a lot," says Miss Peruzzi simply. And being a New Yorker at home with economic facts, she adds, "I think Skally's going to teach in the afternoon study center next term—know what I mean?" Which explains things a bit more. For that is the latest plum at P.S. 200—eleven dollars a night from 3 to 5 P.M., teaching children phonics and the reading they didn't learn during the day. Peruzzi adds "Gee . . . that eleven dollars is a temptation. But Eineman wouldn't, I wouldn't. I mean, you're too tired, if you've had these kids all day." But here Peruzzi has gone far enough. She takes out some red grapes and begins to peel them, then inserts them dreamily, one by one, between her white teeth.

A special new sound is now rising from the far end of the building, a sort of low, distant humming. Traffic boy José

35

Cardona, age eleven, a fat, intellectual boy with solemn smile, appears in the door. He jerks his chin at the corridor: "Gonna be bad today, Miss Burke, Miss Peruzzi, due to the rain. Lotta subs. Get ready."

Peruzzi says across the table, "Let's see the hands, José," and he holds up beautiful, small hands that are so dirty that even washing (I've stood over him while he's washed them) doesn't get the dirt out of the cracks. Every line in the palms is etched in dirt. She had José in second grade, when he first came out of a long stay in Bellevue. She never found out why—he is as easy-going, always talking and chatting with you, as he is alienated—she heard he set things on fire in buildings. He thinks the worst of himself. "I don't get along with kids good," he says. "Oh, listen:" (spittle at his lips) "I'm not goin in the class for two days. The kids are layin low for me." This is not true; the children respect him, but he has few friends. Mrs. Bergens has him in sixth grade now, and sometimes he comes in with a note to me from her about coffee at four. I'll see him washing his hands in the drinking fountain in the corridor before he enters. Loves to stand around interrogating the children while I answer the note. "What book are you reading, children?—Hey, that's all? Primer level in this class?" "Yes, José, unfortunately it's all they can read." "Well, let's play something," he calls out. "Give me the names of two great American writers after 1850 . . . name two works by Mark Twain."

Once, José gave me the names of books that Enrico Fermi had in his library. He pulled a piece of paper out of his shirt pocket, which turned out to be a pajama top—a formula of Fermi's, could I explain it? Once, last term, I went with Mrs. Eineman to his home. She wanted to take him some tangerines. There had been some problem; she was told to send down his class folder, but she could never find out why. In his home he told her, "Oh, I got a home teacher now since I've been in Bellevue. I don't get along with children; you know that, Mrs. Eineman." "That's ridiculous. Who told you that?" He was spending the week-end with his mother and baby sister that day we visited him, in a flat whose walls were a grim but blinding steel blue. We'd walked in on a family quarrel. José had sneaked home to see his family, then refused to go, while his mother pleaded. It was pouring rain outside. He was soaked to the skin— had on pajamas under a leaky raincoat and wouldn't take the raincoat off. He'd say, "Hey, Mom, you know what a pinwheel is? It's an optical illusion if you paint it different colors." "You're supposed to be at Gramma," she would tell him. "No room here." He kept laughing, crying, and refusing to leave. The ninety-pound mother repeated, "No room,

36

José, you a big boy. You must go to Mama." "Listen to that mother of mine, Mrs. Eineman. Hey, what do you think about this hair my sister's got herself?" he laughed, picking up a handful of one child's flaming red hair. "Wild, isn't it? I'll never forget this hair."

"Well, come on, read us the news, José," Miss Peruzzi tells him now and hands him a *Times*. He begins with dramatic pauses, "Heroic Major Gordon Cooper, conqueror of space—oh hey. Listen to that! Must get back to my post!" The distant drone is changing key—an intent muttering now, drawing closer. It's the approach of hundreds of children's feet. It detaches itself suddenly from any organ of sound and bursts into a free rumbling roar.

Lunch cook, a huge Negro woman with arms and hands like oars, materializes at the door to the children's lunchroom. Next to her, Burns, an aide, in the green tam. Only the toughest teachers will take lunchroom duty and few do —even though if you do, you're given a smaller class. The last child to call Burns a fucking bitch will not do so soon again. Burns has lately been put on guard duty and taken on trips. She said, "I went with 'em to that soap factory, but none of 'um knew the capital of New York." Cook is now swinging to and locking the door, so that only a single line can cram through and hurl itself on the food. The roar is rising—claps and crashes mingling into it—they're rounding the stairways. It mounts to a great wave of sound and breaks, lunging with a rush through the gym doors! Cardona disappears; a moment later his traffic badge flings up over the small rushing bodies. "Get back! Get back!" Burns is booming. One great arm becomes a bar to the half-door, the other she uses to encircle with a single flowing movement children who thrash or kick. Does something to the nerve in each child's arm—pinches or deadens it. You can tell it all the way from here—you can hear the yipes and even make out hungry faces bellowing up at her.

We salvage Cardona, help him find his badge and glasses, then for the next few minutes Peruzzi and I chat in low voices under the roar. Between us and the children lies the gym floor decked with basketballs.[4]

[4] Health class has been playing all morning directed by Mr. Zoller, who can't make them put the balls away, and this is our school in a nutshell. This month at practically any minute of the day you can find health classes playing ball in the gym, or the second grade dancing. Last month, in contrast, there were so many meetings—teachers' interest committees, meetings about what door the children would come in, Higher Horizons meetings, Teachers' Luncheon, piñata parties—so much frolicking of every kind going on, the gym had to be locked off for two weeks.

The noise going on behind the closed metal doors of the children's lunchroom is indescribable. Just to give an idea: it takes thirty minutes to feed most of 1200 children. Once fed, they're channeled out the other end onto the street. When Peruzzi and I walk through today, it's empty but a shambles. Only "slow eaters"—fifty or so—are still at tables covered with pools of slopped or hurled pineapple juice, some bloodied. Untouched liverwurst sandwiches are stomped onto the floor, some wrapped in wax paper and never opened. Smashed hard-boiled eggs, puddles of vegetable soup, quarter-oranges trampled into garbage. Sandwiches with holes in them (spit-through-the-hole game), sandwiches packed into baseballs. The slow eaters we pass are small or weak children whose first tray was torn from them. A few are hungry children who'll eat what they do not like. But few will eat carefully these well-balanced meals served to them each day; eight hundred or more, free of charge. "I can't eat sausage; I can't eat dark bread." "I ain't eatin this. I only eat beans, rice, and bananas." "I gonna puke." "My mother lets me drink coffee at home, so why do I have to drink milk here?" Milk once served, opened or not, must be poured out or drunk under the attendants' eyes. It's against the rule to tell a child not to take milk if he won't drink it. All uneaten food, touched or not, must be tossed into garbage cans under attendants' eyes. To exit, you must be in the garbage line. Many children take the tray and dump it without sitting down.

Women at the food end of the room are lugging the giant garbage cans, two women to a can, to the alley doors. Every day when the sanitation trucks have come to pick up, the rows of cans are Lysolized, hosed down, and polished by Puerto Rican women until they shine like silver. In the alley, we pass the first ten: loaded with sandwiches, eggs with one end ripped off, oranges, that taken from P.S. 200 alone would feed fifty people a day. One great can is flowing to the brim with milk. The children tear open the cartons, sip or spit the milk at one another. But they must pour away whatever's left.

Office notices: Last week of the Book Fair. Teaching Career Month. Pan-American Day. "Boys and Girls of Other Lands Week." From the Bureau of In-Service Training: Remember to file applications for salary differentials.

Teachers gathering again. "Sure, it's worth it if you care about culture at all. . . . You get your group of ten or more, group discount—" "Barbra Streisand?" "Yeah, but I don't know, I thought she'd be better than she was. . . .

No, no, she's great—I just thought she'd be better, that's all."
". . . down to Florida over Easter, but could we keep a sun
tan more than a week back here? I hear those Florida tans—"
"Oh, I knew a kid in college kept a real even deep tan year
round, she'd just fly down to Florida in vacation and keep it
up with a sunlamp." "Yeah, but I have a funny kind of skin."
Mrs. Moss found someone for lunch, though it was only
Mrs. Rudge.

MOSS. Mar-velous Picasso show on Fifty-seventh. I was
fortunate enough to go with a very dear old friend of mine;
it was an emotional catharsis. I love Picasso; if they were
showing Picasso in Jersey, I'd go to Jersey; if Brooklyn,
Brooklyn, but I will say frankly—

RUDGE. Yeah, I don't blame you, you feel that way about it.

MOSS. Well, what do you feel? About Picasso?

RUDGE. Well, I like Picasso, sure, but—

MOSS. Like? That's no way to talk about Picasso. Listen,
I've always been interested in the arts—

RUDGE. Yeah, I can see your point. I don't blame you.

Mrs. Feldman, a former teacher, now a supervisor, has been
waiting at my mailbox. I was trying to see Zang again. She
is deeply distressed that I'm not going to Europe this summer.
Can she be of assistance in obtaining a bank loan? "If you
are setting forth to that matchless continent, there is a certain
aggregate that is entailed. . . ." In this same manner Mrs.
Feldman addresses the fourth grade if she enters my room.
The children stare at her elegant blue-tinted hair; they listen
to the low melodic voice that seems to them to come from
some long-ago fairyland: ". . . to grow up in the United
States, to devolve from childish idleness into the heritage of
thoughtful citizenship, we must apply ourselves diligently,
boys and girls, through childhood as at every other period, to
the problems at hand. I do not expect, boys and girls, when
next I may have reason to enter this room, to see confusion
and chaos. . . ."

PART II

Harlem

1

RICHARD. I saw realll dinosaurs at the World's Fair. They now distinct, and they had wings and little claws.

CHILDREN. Teacher, he wasn't at no Fair. He just storyin and you don't know it.

RICHARD. I did so see 'em! *Long* before I was in this school.

(A fight is starting.)

TEACHER. Let's think about turtles. Remember the sea turtle who comes out of the sea and lays eggs—where?

MONTY. In the sand, and the hot sun pops 'em open! And the children turtles has to make it to the sea all by theirselves. But the children gets up and walks down to that old sea when they ready.

TEACHER. But how do they know where the sea is, and when it's time?

CHILDREN. They *knows*. They just knows!

LEANORE (seated by front desk, she rises, about to knock book from desk she's so angry). Those mothers are not gonna leave those babies.

VERNON. Dumb girl, them mothers have *nothin* to do with them baby eggs.

LEANORE. Would not leave those babies!

RUBY. Better than turtles I like penguins. They keeping each other warm in the *cold*—stands shoulder to shoulder.

RICHARD. Bracing the storm.

MALCOLM. They stays in that dark for months!

JOSIE. Oh, I be so afraid in the dark!

REGGIE. Not me, boy, I'd love the South Pole, I'd slide everywhere like crazy on that ice; I'd *twirrrlll* around in that old flying snow with my mouth open, throw me great snowballs. . . . Run and run!

VERNON. That *blizzard* scares me, but I loves that snow!

RICHARD. And the penguin mates sinnng to each other!

VERNON. That bird *ain't really a bird*.

OTHERS. You kiddin, it is a true bird! They can't fly, but they can swimmmm!

JOSIE. I loves when you reads about penguins, but I don'ts believe in them.

CASSANDRA. I never go out my house when Joe the Indian's there. He live in back, he don't want truck with black children. Light color he like, not my color. My sister, she light color. Joe don't want me in the hall when he come out.

ERNIE. Your *brother* black. He mean and black.

CASSANDRA. Don't call him that!

CURTIS. Well, you a coal-black sea-hag! *Double* coal-black sea-hag!

(Teacher approaching classroom.)

WILLIAM. Here come the white cracker!

From the first day: "Don' *touch* me." "Don' you white touch me." Josie: "I loves the way your hands match, top and bottom, that's really good. But you gets so *crazy* white when you get mad. I can't *stand* it."

Touch a boy's wrist saying "Your sleeve's unbuttoned," he shrinks back. He wipes his wrist off. Don't—for weeks—guide hands in handwriting.

42

MALCOLM. They playin kick-the-can, loadies, they leaves me out, I'm too bright-colored. They get so made at me, even though I'm colored—they say, "Hey, you looks like a white boy!" But I'm colors too! I tells them I am!

VERNON. Why your hair that color?

TEACHER. It's the kind of hair I have, that's all.

VERNON. That hair just ain't real.

RICHARD. Listen, all you need is *pomade*. I'm gonna bring some, fix that hair up. My hair just as soft as yours when I gots my pomade on.

There is no such thing as quiet. Feet pound and scramble in halls outside all day. Racket through vent of Mr. Goff's room—banging, scraping all day, something like sawing and chopping, but it's not a C.R.M.D. class.

Strict guard. Aides $1.65 an hour (straight lines to the *Amsterdam News*). No one is to enter without a pass, but they do. Police visit in the afternoons; mothers and relatives of children mill around in the entrance hall from 2:30 on. Mothers slip up to rooms. Older brothers and sisters drop in to "visit." Sixth-grade children race up and down halls and boxed stairways, cut, scud, slide, and shriek in and out of stair doors and halfway landings and turns. Surges of girls upon the washrooms—shriek and gone, shriek and gone. From inside washrooms (heartbeat of the school), deep, pleasurable laughing floats out—then this erupts into brawls. Doors along the hall are shut for protection but pulled open by the waves of running kids. Open the door a moment, all kids in the room stand up to hear—constant gravitation, inside, to the bodies rushing outside. After twenty minutes a teacher may come out into the hall to round up the two who've gone to the washroom, discover eight others. Lull for a few moments. Then a new surge.

Stairway windows: back sides of tenements swoop from holes at the bottom where garbage rots or smolders, up to the roofs where junkies go. A brassiere dropped from a washline to hook itself on a telephone pole—a joke for a week, as lines of kids move up and down the stairs. "Hey, there she still is!"

This is third exponent (a class grouping according to reading level) of fourth grade. Four good readers (Richard, Reggie, Leanore, Virgil)—second-grade level. Three at first grade, the rest primer. Four absolute nonreaders. All are fifth-grade age.

Many are disturbed, seven severely. Fifteen or more have asthmatic attacks. Ten thumbsuckers. Any diversion, as little as change of subject—everybody in back stands up and starts talking.

Some children fall asleep two or three times a day. Teachers cannot determine why in each case—malnutrition, fatigue, stress. The ones not sleeping squirm, hang over their desks, call across the room to their friends. Coats often pulled over their heads. Others keep coats on chair backs all day. The building's so old, the coat closet is jammed and no one can be found to fix it. So it's easy to grab your coat and run.

At the first PTA no mothers came, but fifteen did to Mrs. Hervine's room (top exponent of fourth grade). Mrs. Weiss, supervisor, says this is much the same everywhere. Generally, the children whose parents come will go on, through junior high and high school.

Mr. Saltz, the principal, is good. Orthodox views but he does walk the halls and goes into classrooms all day. Mrs. Weiss: "Don't expect too much. He has to keep clean with the neighborhood. Every now and then he gets calls—pols. or the *Amsterdam News*. Yes, often back of that is one of our teachers. Plenty of disaffection here. When that happens, he gets shaky and won't talk to anyone for a few days."

We send down for 1.1 (first grade, first semester) readers but there aren't any. The book room sends up 2.1, hoping we can make out. Math book is fourth grade. No phonics book. No math workbook. No beadboards. No alphabet cards, and they don't know what comes before *i* when they alphabetize. They need simple dictionaries. Mrs. Weiss says supply money goes into replacing books that get lost or destroyed.

JOSIE

Fat and sleepy. Number nine in a family of thirteen, sleeps with three of the babies. Much coming and going of adults in her home—not fathers but Arthur, Harris, etc. Admires her friend Leanore who can read and has a grip on things. Can't read a word herself but advises me on everything.

TEACHER. How does Curtis spell his last name, *ph* or *f?* He's been gone two days; his papers have three different spellings. I have to send down a 407 on him.

JOSIE. If I was you, I'd send down a 407 on Reginald.

TEACHER. That's for hooky players.

JOSIE. I don't care. A 407 gets action. (Working busily.)
Do you know, I likes to make *w*'s. I think that my favorite
letter. I gots to complete this, then I taken me a book home
today.

CURTIS

> (Curtis has just grabbed his coat and run out.)

RICHARD. You know how nuts I am? Well, *Curtis—!* In first
grade he used to kick the teacher, make her leg black and
blue, or he'd *ram* his head into her.

CHILDREN. Oh, he's always running away, he got put outta
four rooms last year.

CURTIS (outside). You watch your tongues! I'll pop you in
your mouth. Why don't you talk about your own self sometime?

RICHARD. Been stealing candy money off little kids since
first grade, but he goes craaazy when sixth-graders shakes *us*
down!

RUBY. He stoled twenty-five dollars from Mr. Goff last year!

RICHARD. Yesterday he was cuttin that biiiig cake with a
ruler down in reading, wouldn' give no one a piece and
that was stolen cake. Only gives away stuff he has to get rid
of fast. Red and yellow masks, he stoled them at Blumstein's,
give them away to sixth-grade boys!

MONTY. And money! He's got money on him now, I saw
quarters shine.

A daily routine. Grabs his coat and runs. He may get out
of the building; or hang around in the hall to stick his head
in with big pouts, or shrill "Liars!" Loves having someone
come out and drag him back in. Or sweet talk may get him
back in about twenty-five minutes on his terms: "I'll come in
if Noah quit bothering me, but I won't do the math, past
page thirty-five, and I wanta finish weaving my potholder,
then finish my painting of George Washington. . . ." Try to
grab him, he runs off and plays down the hall with other
kids who've left other rooms to play.

He goes from mood to mood; he seems to have no sub-
stance. On his second-grade record someone wrote "has a

sweet streak in him." And I've seen him walk back to a new boy, Ernie, and explain the set-up of the room: "You got to keep your papers in order and don't lie to her. Don't think she'll give up on anything; it's best just give in the first time. If you lie, she'll have you stay till you tell the truth."

Often he's not sure what the problem is until we clash over folding a paper in thirds or quarters. Or he'll be sitting quietly, cleaning out his notebook, putting all the yellow papers together—a clash, he's ruined for the day. "You like to paint Washington—, don't you want to read about him too? You *must* learn to read." He'll turn on me a look of strange candor: "I'm sick of reading, of the whole school if you want to know. Reading's a stupid game. I'm not gonna play it."

Mr. Goff, who had him last year, says, "Yeah, he's sweet like a rotten apple is. Look, I don't mean to discourage you, but he just wants *out*. He's too old to change now. Nothing behind him at home. His mother adores him, neglects the other kids for him. Look at how he's dressed—a prince. But I don't want to talk about the kid. He's a bad egg."

Taken to the acting principal, Mr. Ferré, for tearing a book apart, Curtis easily charms the adult with his childish downcast giggle. Ferré is confused. "Well, you see, now you're smiling . . . you can't be such a bad boy after all."

TEACHER. Please come in this afternoon, Curtis. We're going to do math, and you're *so* good in math, we need you. You're not a terribly good reader just now, but who's good in arithmetic, Curtis? Who's the very *best* in arithmetic? All right, will that person please come in?

VERNON. Better come in, man, she gettin mad.

CURTIS. Tell her she can come out and get me. (Calls in) Oh, you think you're so great, bossing us from up there, tell me I can't write in a library book, you don't own that library even if you think you do.

If I come in I'm not gonna do the math; I'll do the addition but not the subtraction but I'm gonna paint Washington and I'm not coming in. If you wanted me to come in, you wouldn't have said those things to me you did yesterday. Why don't you get your lies straight? Yesterday you said it took me thirty minutes to do math; today you told Mr. Ferré it took twenty-five minutes. You talk a lot, I notice that about you. No, don't tell me you're gonna call my mother. You keep saying you're gonna do that but you don't do it, so why keep saying it? And don't think about seeing her, save yourself a trip, my mother doesn't care anyway.

Half an hour later, he slips in to get his coat. Further dialogue; a chase around the room. Suddenly, I hand him the coat—also a wrong move. Noah is now walking out of the room, Josie is throwing hair oil on the floor and weeping, and in a flash Curtis is gone.

ROGER

Has never laughed. Stares, doesn't blink. Moves fast or not at all.

Teacher: "Stand up if you did not do your homework." Roger shoots up out of his seat, shivering his head—the only one, though seven did no homework. Doesn't know why he didn't. Shakes his head, eyes fixed.

He has just laid a work paper on the desk. Teacher (glancing over it): "Why, this is a very good alphabetized paper, Roger." His eyes follow mine and the paper's surface. He is murmuring some indistinct words like ". . . paper . . . not . . ."

"Roger, I can't quite hear you." His eyes are engulfing the paper. He says something like ". . . in the middle . . . with? . . ." Reaches up one of his strange elderly hands, touches an edge. "Roger, is it something about your name? The heading?" His knuckle points to the middle of the paper, withdraws, moves off the paper. He whispers ". . . in the middle? . . ."

Lately, he's been sending up to the desk rather good drawings of birds in care of Harold, a trusted boy who sits next to him. Yesterday a drake with stretched wings appeared, then the American eagle in profile wreathed with stars. There is nothing to do but give Harold the message, "Tell him this bird is beautiful." Harold goes back to waiting Roger. Harold speaks, Roger starts with shocked, vivid, silent smile.

In reading he jumps when called on and reads rapidly in a high voice, not what's on the page but something similar to the reading of a few days ago. A new story in his own words: "Eagle is a good boy who helps his mother, he shifts the canoe down into the water, he paddles to the winter camp." Children are crying "Whaatt?" and Harold leans over to check the page, but no, Roger is on the right page, finger on the starting word. He continues, "Eagle looks for the blue sky of spring and he hopes—"

Arithmetic: "One and one are—?" "Two . . ." "Good. One and one *and one?*—" ". . . T-t-two? . . ." "No, watch

47

my fingers, Roger. How many fingers?" (One finger is held up.) "One? . . ." (A second is held up.) "That is—?"
". . . T-t-t- . . . ten?"

MONTY (LAMONT)

He can read. But spasms interrupt his work all day. His shoulders throw apart violently, head jerks back as though a snake runs through him. Once he screamed, then covered his head with his coat.

Mr. Goff: "You must insist that a neurologist see this child. He used to scream last year from pains in his head."

"I did send him to Guidance; they sent for the mother. She didn't come."

"Well . . . you'll have to keep trying."

WILLIAM

WILLIAM. Y'all push this work on me too fast, I am 'tarded.

CHILDREN. Yes, he's 'tarded, teacher!

RUBY. He is 'tarded. Miss Guernsey said that in second grade. She said in some ways he was a blessing, other ways a curse.

(Unprecedented racket outside, sounds of battle, flying feet, etc.)

TEACHER. Shut the door, Vernon. Those must be some re-tarded children.

CHILDREN. No, you wrong, you so wrong. It's Mr. Rowby's sixth grade, they gonna see a parade!

NOAH. Mr. Rowby plays with his mustache all day.

JASON. Mr. Rowby swings and balls Mrs. Merck!

RICHARD. Listen, when that 'tarded class go by, you realllly know it.

VERNON. I won't be here this afternoon, I'm going down to help the 'tarded children, don't mark me absent.

TEACHER. Just be back here at one as usual, Vernon.

VERNON. No, I gotta go down and help out.

RUBY. Before you got to be our teacher, we didn't have a steady teacher and we help out down there sometimes. It was just *too much!* I couldn't have a room like that, all the papers flying—teacher, you'd have one of your best fits if you saw that class.

JOSIE. But I never swo' when I was down there. It so sad to be 'tarded, they gots the 'tarded children a 'tarded teacher to make them happy.

RUBY. The 'tarded teacher don't seem to think they can be lined up in twos like we got in this class. They got all the wrong feets in wrong shoes, and they spits *so much* water.

JOSIE. They spits all over. I didn't bring my raincap, but honest, I could have used it. She let them do *anything.* It's better if you works in first grade.

VERNON. Nobody ever sits down, ever! You gots to pin everything on you. I passed out paper for orange pumpkins down there last week and they's two doors there. The children comes in and out in circles! I say, "Didn't I just give you a orange paper?" I can't tell which is who, they comin in and out so fast in circles, and she sayin, "Everybody in now because I'm going to pass out paste."

REGGIE. I gots so mixed up by two, I quit.

TEACHER. Where did you go?

REGGIE. Home.

At noon, the teen-agers pile out of Jefferson Junior High, two blocks north, and pile up in gangs on the street. Men on construction crews for the new school keep silent (they don't want trouble), as gangs explode in screaming, "Mothehfuck!" mad laughing, cigarettes lighting and stabbing at each other. Mobs of girls cut the rest of the day and turn up in our elementary building to visit former teachers or go down and help in C.R.M.D. rooms or first grade. At three, out pours the rest of Jefferson. More gangs appear across the street; within minutes boys shove into girl gangs, smoking madly, whistling and calling, books bouncing high. They hang over construction machinery and ripped-up pavement. You can hear them over the pile drivers.

Around the building, Jefferson beats and swings. The beat builds up. Stairs and washrooms take over the building. Motors charging. Boys stream up and down stairs. Other boys yell and charge the girls' washroom each time sixth-grade girls move in. Boys shove up against the door, peering in through the hole, girls screaming, "You get 'way, boy, this ain't to do with you!" "What you want, boy, get outta here!" Sometimes a plaintive cry, "Get out, Mickey, or I tell Mr. Ferré."

Lily of fifth grade whines around outside the door: "Teacher, you know what Curtis say to me? He wantsa piece. You know what he wants a piece of, teacher?"

CURTIS. That's a dirty lie, shut you' lying mouth, bitch!

LILY. Don't you wanta know what he wanta piece of, teacher?

LEANORE

She was sent to a special Home in second grade for starting a serious fire in her building. Tall—a head above the others —willowy. Clothes with labels of Lord & Taylor, other good stores—worn by someone before her but always just out of the cleaner. Sits in a dead calm, talking to herself for an hour. Then a whirr of activity: stands up to call insults over the room, head thrown back, with rippling laughs. Slams her desk, takes coat, walks out.

She and Josie talk silly things, call back and forth all day.

JOSIE. You leave her alone, woman. She is showin me something.

TEACHER. Sit down.

LEANORE. I don't wanta sit down; he's got my coat, he's got my ruler. Listen, he thinks he can take that good ruler my mother paid fifty cents for, he's crazy and you're crazy too. I'll sit down when I'm good and ready. You better not come near me. Watch that coat, lady!

TEACHER. Hang up the coat. It's only one-thirty.

LEANORE. You better not touch this coat.

TEACHER. Sit down.

LEANORE. I'm borrowing a sheet of paper—you want me to do that work or not? I'm not gonna do it anyway, and I'm not putting a heading on it. What page is this? What's that say up there on the blackboard?

(A ruler rises in air to draw a line between her and path to blackboard.)

50

Watch out that ruler! That ruler come *near* my eyelash—

TEACHER. Leanore, you look so beautiful today. (Sincere compliment, and trying to get her to drift into her seat.) What's that, a bouffant hairdo?

LEANORE. You kiddin, my sister burnt this hair—it *was* supposed to be a bouffant. If I get her, I'll kill her; this ain't no bouffant.

(Later. Class writing. Calls out:)

I'm getting this hair braided tomorrow. Or plaited, as my mother calls it. Yes, if you like a big word, by all means say *plait*. My mother wants no one but her touching this hair. This hair is freshly plaited daily; she is having a hard time with this hair. She wants it to grow, plaits it very sharply, so it'll *really* last, four or five days. Then Shirley Temple curls, soon.

JOSIE. Girl, you can't get Shirley Temple curls, your hair's way too short. You should get an African Girl.

LEANORE. My mother gets hers set in a parlor, hot oil to make it nice. And I am too. She's takin me to a dance this week-end; nothing will stop that. I'm wearing shoes with a small heel and my loveliest dress with the silk panels. A white velvet band in my hair.

(Later. New clear, loud pitch.)

You gets a mother bird some time, she'll get a hatchet and cut up anything she find and feed each kid bird.

ERNEST. Where'd she get a hatchet?

(Leanore laughs and springs across room, hits William who's bent in a V looking at underside of his seat, flies back to her seat, scattering papers. Stares at pages of her book. Lets them flutter.)

(Quiet reading period. Her voice turns on, like a phonograph:)

Pah-pah-pah-pah . . . camas roots, camas roots, camas roots, Indian, Indian, Eagle, Eagle, Eagle tepee, camas roots, Indian mother, tepee, Indian mother, Indian boys.

(Dashes out the door at 2:00 P.M. An aide searches but Leanore hides in the girls' washroom, then sneaks out to hide in stairwell landings. Class continues. She

runs back and forth outside, spitting water through rent
in the door, panting, calling in:)

Who's afraid of the big bad teacher? Not Le-a-nore! Tee-
hee! (Runs off. Imitates teacher) Boys and girls take out
your books! Put away your books. Take out your pencils!
Put away your paper! Tee-hee! Anyone who has not read in
this room today, watch out! (Steps run off. Run back. Spits
water through the hole. Imitates) Mop up that water! (Imitates
a bass voice) Wil-liam wants to put his hand in Cassie's pants
but (imitates teacher) "We-don't-do-that-in-this-room!" (Bass
voice again) Ruby's got herself a head full of blaaack wooollly
hair and she is soooo black! Ernie's mother has so many holes
in her drawers, she don't know which ones to put her legs
through. Hee-hee-hee! (Normal voice, in rage) Woman, you
gimme that dictionary!

(Class continues.)

My father'll come and cut you up. . . . I'll take your coat.
. . . I'll take your purse. . . . I've *got* to have that dictionary;
gimme that dictionary; I can't go home without it.
    Next day, Leanore does not come back from lunch. Just
opens the door, calls in "Stupid!" a couple of times, disappears.

JOSIE

Lives in the building next to Leanore. "Leanore's with Miss
Caroline this week," says someone. "No, chil'," says Josie.
"That's Leanore's mother. *Miss Octavia,* Leanore's grandmother, where she is now. . . . Miss Octavia lives in a hotell
where they changes the sheets every Friday, and you gots
to pay weekly for the television. When she move in, Leanore
help her, live with her for a week. They are twin beds in
that room, and Leanore go there *any time* she can'ts be at
home.
    "Leanore be getting a awful beating last night. She probably
be gone a few days now. Sidney came down that street
last night. He don't even belong in this neighborhood, but
sometimes he be coming up here just like he *do,* and her
mother and sisters be *scream*-in at each other, but he just
passes 'em *all* by!"

MALCOLM. That Miss Caroline she is baaad! That whole
family gets out in that street. Miss Caroline standing there
and Leanore's sisters are screaming; then her sisters raise

bottles. And the father pretend he don't see any of them, slip in that tavern; but her mother shoot right in after him!

JOSIE. Sidney not Leanore's father, he's the baby's father. Arthur is Leanore's father.

(The street scene is played over with other speakers.)

JOSIE. When we had the other teacher, Leanore's mother come one day and were *so* mad. Jason had tore Leanore's coat. Miss Caroline come in the afternoon and cursed the teacher and say, "No chil' here better ever touch that *mouth* of Leanore. *Stay away from that mouth.* I got five hundred dollars worth of steel in there. Hands off my baby's mouth, anybody touch that mouth they go down to Twenty-third Street District so fast your head'll spin, I knows that judge. I don't intend to get to the bottom of this coat stuff right this minute, but I *will;* meantime don't no one lay hand on that mouth. Watch it, Mr. Jason, 'less your mother can get up five hundred dollars! Bet your sweet life she can't."

Josie's junior-high sister comes in with the two o'clock Jefferson tide and says, "Yuh, okay, teacher," popping gum in my ear as I explain simple homework for her to show Josie. Josie's mother shows up a night later. A slight smile plays in the corners of her mouth. "Real-ly like you givin Josie this help, but I hope you don't try to take her off me. Miss Thayer tried doin that; she babied Alberta from fourth grade on. Oh, yes. Used to take her home to her nice house, spent all that time and money on Alberta; now Alberta sorry she had all that truck with Miss Thayer. Now Alberta say *her own* mother's the best over anyone. . . ."

The sister turns up in the halls on Friday, two friends at her side carrying big stacks of messy books and notebooks, cheeks chewing and throbbing. Teachers get so they don't ask these teen-agers questions. Anything triggers them. "Huh-yuh, Josie's teacher, how's Josie doin'?" "Why fine, you've really been helping Josie. She shows it; keep it up." The girl friends smile. But they're waiting for it. One of them—the pause has been too long—tilts forward, grins. "Say, Miss . . . say . . . what color you call that hair?" The sister just cuts it off—steps back on her friend's toes. The friend snickers but shuts up. For this time.

CURTIS

The pattern that has been set in the room is not going down to lunch until work is completed. Every child now conforms to this. Curtis does not. He sneaks out and sneaks

53

back forty minutes late. This time he sees Malcolm waiting.

MALCOLM.   Come on in, Curtis, I'm gonna beat your face. Gimme back my fifty cents you stole. You been smoking cigarettes with the fifth-grade boys at Mickey's, that's why you're late.

CURTIS.   Dirty lie, you weren't there. Don't butt in other people's business!

MONTY.   Whooo! Man, your father'll bang you up against that wall tonight!

Curtis is choking with anger but tries to sneak in for the coat. Malcolm jumps him, filthy fight, heads pounding on the floor. Fight ends down at principal's office, Curtis sent home with a lady aide and a note. In talking with the principal, I use the words "a very disturbed child."

Mr. Saltz: "Now, just a moment. Neither you nor I are ever qualified to call a child disturbed. I'll mention this to Guidance again . . . but there's nothing in his record to indicate violence, you see."

Curtis is missing for a week this time. Mr. Goff says, "The stepfather probably beat him but not for stealing. The beatings don't really mean anything. Nothing does that happens to him. And he won't bother the mother being home; she's ginned up most of the time, anyway. Look, he's fair-skinned; he's smart. He's the apple of that family's eye."

Monty says, "I think he come back maybe, but I don't know. He jus' sittin at home on that ol' bed of his, doin nothin."

Homes

Jason is the only one with a father who has a steady job. "My father a doctor, he takes care of washing all the walls in the operating room at Metropolitan Hospital. Those walls got to be *perfect;* there can't be a single germ." Leanore's father is a truck driver; he comes over when her mother is in the hospital or jail. Richard's father is in Florida, "But he gonna come up and get me." There are no other fathers that anyone knows about.

They have mothers, sometimes a stepfather, grandmothers. Some mothers do menial work two or three afternoons a week in white homes across Central Park.

54

Brothers and Sisters

The smallest family in the room is four, most others are families of seven and eight children. A dozen children have older brothers at home who've dropped out of school anywhere from seventh grade on. Josie is number nine of thirteen and is ten years old—her mother had her first baby at fifteen. Four have older sisters, now pregnant in their early teens. Often my children become foster mothers of their mothers' babies. Josie comes in one morning an hour late. "I'se got to be the mother now, teacher. I'se ten. Just like my mother when she were little. She tol' me to get foods today, gives me ten dollars, and I got Tide, red rice, five chickens, five pounds of onions, 'nanas. She had to be mother, and boil the clothes when she were ten."

CASSANDRA. Oh, my stepfather come over last night and were *so* mean, call me Black Sambo, and goes in my mother's puh'se. Says, "Oh Harriet, now I owe you $10.19," then a little later say, "Harriet I owe you $12.37 now." And he got *no* mind to pay any of it back. I always goes out and say, "Mama, he in your puh'se." But I don't look at him much. And I gots my own bed and sleeps with no other puh'son. My mother's on my side, I know that. And my grandmother always say, "Cassie, you come down here any time. Bring a few things."

RUBY. Oh, they fussin bad at *my* house last night. My grandmother come get us. But my sister won't leave. That baby *love* to get in on the action.

VERNON. My grandmother gone back down south and took my brother. He just couldn't be in New York no more. And my grandmother got a workhorse; my brother rides it!

NOAH. Down south you gets whupped with a hose, you acts up in school. If you gets drunk on Sunday, the police lock you up. And you can't do the Dog, or Monkey, or Frug on Sunday. My father hates that about the South.

(Interruptions: "What part South you talkin about, boy?" "You sure can dance in *my* South on Sunday.")

NOAH. Maybe in Bamba you can dance; not my South.

OTHERS. Well, I sure don't know what South *you* is.

VERNON. My grandmother handles things *southern*. My sister stole that wallet from Blumstein's: well, my father give
me the wallet to punish my sister; my grandmother make me
take it back. She push you right in Blumstein's if you steal,
make you handle it yourself. If they see me put it back, they
gonna think *I took it*. I say to her, "I'll throw it on the
floor." But she don't care; she say, "I'm just gonna *throw
you* in that sto'." She don't know about these things; she
southern. Our super always try to curse her out about her
dog. But she say, no small dog's gonna make a big dog's
mess. Speak up in a nice way, to that super.

JASON. Listen, child, in the South the coloreds and whites
be friends but not up here. You can set around and laaaugh
with those white peoples down there! Not here. No one minds
nothin up here. Everything different up here.

Josie learns some sight words, and for a reward I take her
to midtown Manhattan to see the sights of Broadway and
eat Chinese food. She has never been out of Harlem. At
Herald Square she asked, "Is this where they goin. to be
elephants? I think this where elephants lives." In a penny
arcade we had our pictures taken. She is a strange little girl,
who chose the snapshot to take home which was the best one
of me, not herself. We went into a big drugstore, and she
spent the time while I was making a phone call hanging
around a counterful of toy mechanical animals. She wound
up each animal, replaced each key, and when all the animals
had been wound up said, "There." It was hard to get her
away from a Horn & Hardart's window where a golden brown
plastic turkey was enthroned among glistening vegetables.
"That turkey do be *so* plump . . . I 'spect he plump enough
to feeds ten children in a family. . . ."
    Later, over ice-cream sodas: "My brother Harvey, he sho
would love that plump turkey. He is *so greedy* with turkey.
He home now, can't wait to Thursday to stuff hisself; he
love a plump bird."
    "Oh, was that Harvey in your hallway when I came by to
get you?"
    "No, that not Harvey. Harvey were inside; that jus' an
addic'," she says dreamily over her ice cream.
    "The addic's stays in the hall now, and I *runnn* when I
sees them! They do be scary. Those addic' takes a scratchy
thing, a pin. First they has to put the pin in a match to kill
germs. Then they puts the pin in their bein."

—Oh, Leanore just story and story you. First she be *mirthful;* then she story and won't stop. She say, "See this person, that my cousin Miss May Belle." But Miss May Belle *my* cousin. Miss May Belle ain't nothin to Leanore. She shouldn't *say* like that, "Miss May Belle my cousin."

JOSIE.   She can think up anything.

RUBY.   Start storyin in Miss Myles' class but Miss Myles said right off, "No crap in here."

JOSIE.   If you puts a hammer to Leanore's knee at that clinic, that *knee don't jump.* There somethin wrong there.

CASSANDRA.   She *cast her spell.* Till my sister say, "No more, Leanore." Besides which, my mother don't want her in our house too much. My mother say, "You sure know when she's here"—ain't that right, Iris?

IRIS.   Sho' is.

RUBY.   Boys try to beat up Leanore after school some days, but she a mean dirty fighter herself; throws they hats and ties on the roof! Then calls her mother Miss Caroline and she come get in on it. That woman's *dangerous.* But Leanore gets mad if someone pick on *you,* you don't punch back for yourself.

CASSANDRA.   My mother say, "Best have everything you wants out of the way when Leanore come, because she tuk everything." She tuk our eggbeater. My mother say, "What kinda child is this, would tuk an eggbeater?"

JOSIE.   She is stayin with Miss Octavia now.

LEANORE AND MISS BOWSER

(The class is preparing to go down to a special assembly for Veterans' Day.)

LEANORE.   Teacher, Curtis is spittin water! If he spits on my good dress, I'll kill him. Teacher, William is trying to steal your pencil: Curtis's trying to get my quarter; Jason's tryin to pick up my dress!

(Runs out, slams door, calls in, comes in, throws papers, runs out.)

VERNON. That girl is greased lightening!

LEANORE (appearing at first stair landing). Josie, stand up straight! Teacher says stand up straight! THERE WILL BE NO TALKING IN LINE! Ha-ha! Ho-ho!

(Disappears around bend. Fifth graders crack-the-whip through our lines: "Kill her! Get her!")

In auditorium, Leanore does falsetto-bass imitations of Miss Currie for some minutes. Then Miss Bowser walks down aisle and pulls Leanore from under a seat.

BOWSER. Just come on here to Miss Bowser, dear. Thaaat's right. What's your name, dear? Oh, I've been watching you for daaays. . . . I think your teacher's being too nice to you.

LEANORE. Let go my arm! I mean it, let go that arm; I'll tell my mother; let go, you big black teacher.

BOWSER. Obey, little girl. Staaand still. (Applies fingers skillfully to Leanore's shoulder.) Yes . . . thaaat's better. Miss Bowser gets obeyed. No, don't twist, lady. (Leanore has given a soft shriek.) I think I'm going to bor-row you a day or two from your teacher, dear. Let's see if we can't iron you out and give you back *pressed* to her.
(To me) We'll try three days. These bitchy little girls can eat you up.

Through the rest of Veterans' Day Assembly Leanore at Miss Bowser's side did not make a move. Mr. Ferré told about the 82nd Airborne Division in World War II (he does this each week), and the children fell asleep, then woke up again when Miss Lamb's grade did the "Grave of the Unknown Soldier" because they like to see who's got what part. There were just two parts: a boy in Cub Scout uniform who was the Grave, and five other children who advanced across the stage, wearing breast bands whose borders had been treated by Miss Lamb's pinking shears, to honor the Grave by presenting plastic tulips. The boy received the tulips in his arms, then turned to the right and bowed his head. The group of five turned in the opposite direction, pressing hands across eyes and looking down. Miss Lamb (you can't mention prayer in a public school): "We all know what they're doing now."

(Later. Back in the room.)

CHILDREN. Oh, Miss Bowser *take care* of Leanore. There's no fussin in Miss Bowser's room. She is a very fat, tough teacher. She and Miss Myles are most tough in this school. Miss Bowser say, "You be good to me, I'll be good to you." But it don't always work that way.

JOSIE. She be turning their arm up their back, and *great pain*.

MISS LAMB

Christian Scientist. A reader in her church. Always has on a nice hat, Cuban heels, a small cross. Six two-piece suits, nice blouses. Dead serious and straight. Always trying to get Miss Bowser up to lead Assembly. Likes talking to new teachers. "Maybe I'll learn something from these young girls just out of teachers' college; I like to keep up." Old-fashioned teacher whose fourth-grade room has homilies and rules ("What a Gentleman Is." "Procrastination is the thief of time." "Our goal for the week.") on the board.

Third- to fourth-floor stair wall is a long seriograph of sex drawings and information about sixth-graders and teachers, ranging from word combinations and messages (fuck, pussy, dick) to complete reports. Our line is coming up from Assembly. The name *Miss Lamb* suddenly flashes out from passing penciled stream! Fast-reading Reggie mutters, *"Miss Lamb!"* straining to catch it, but it slips behind him. Reggie: "Man, that be written fast!"

MR. ROWBY

Stair wall: "Mr. Rowby has a big banana and he can't get enough of Betty Jane's ass (6-A)."

Under thirty. Round, pale face, defeated eyes. When you enter, you know his room is supplied out of his own pocket with many maps, colored chalks, and the like, but the class —this was Mr. Zimmer's class last year; it was in order—this year is a zoo. He believes in one-to-one contact, in trying to reach them all. But being a nice guy is equated with soft. A kid steals money off Rowby's desk. Rowby: "Why did you steal it? I'd have given it to you."

Mrs. Weiss: "He wants to be liked. He has a scene going showing fishes he's brought in, writing instructions on the board, or watering plants but doesn't know what he *should* be doing. I said, 'If children have a seat, they must be in it. I taught fifth grade here last year. I had children who never, not once, swore at me.' He said, 'But all children do.' I said, 'No, they do in your room because you permit it. . . .' "

Children: "The kids in Mr. Rowby's room be warring *everybody,* because they don't know what to do with theirselves. They war so bad, even they gets wore out!"

MRS. ARNHEIM

Mr. Rowby's opposite, teaching a top sixth grade. An intense and disciplined person. Young, under thirty, but dedicated to her vocation. Her children show it.

On her own time last summer, she tutored a little girl who'd failed her class in June; arranged for Rhonda to be re-examined at summer's end, and the child passed at grade level. (Rhonda's mother had come out of prison, and promised to visit the child each week while on parole but didn't.) The tutoring, a daily two or three hours in the park, may have made all the difference.

Mrs. Arnheim goes to NYU classes at night; she's getting her M.A. in elementary teaching. She does psychological testing with children on her own time. She lunches with two or three children downstairs each day. In her top fifth-grade room is a bright library table, with new books each week; a science display she and children have cooperatively prepared. Her children learn quietly and steadily. On Assembly day, they appear with starched clean blouses and walk with their heads up.

———————

Thanksgiving approaches. Mr. Rowby grows pale, seems ill, but stays in school; other teachers absent. Double number of substitutes, and assistant principals taking over classes on every floor. By Wednesday the building is turning over. Guys tumbling in and out of washrooms, "Shi', man, don't push this door," fights, rushes on girls' washrooms, girls' screams. A girl is grabbed, carried halfway down the hall, her friends pile out and rescue her; they get back in the washroom, more screams. Boards in the door slip. Water floods and fights. Mr. Rodgers, the janitor, scrubs new outbursts of signs from stair walls, some in red Magic Marker: "Mr. Pressman so busy gettin pusy he don't have time to give out homework." "Mr. Ferré is a A.M. man." "Relish think he's fine but wait till he see Butch." "Someone is a pussy lover that is in class 6.4." (Added: "Pussy is bad." Added: "Talk for yourself.") "Miss Griffin really *throws* her ass around."

Jefferson invasions and ambushes; boys with silk stockings on their heads, yelling in wolf-packs across street; girls in avocado storm coats, puffing clouds of smoke around their heads. A boy pulls a cigarette from his mouth at the door: "Hey man, when this fuckin school gonna let out, hey?" to a male sub.

Some teachers give little parties in their rooms. All say they never will again. Mr. Saltz sent a notice around, "All parties to start at 1:30 but not before." Most rooms are parties all day. Mrs. Weiss saw the 'Tarded Teacher hauling two great bags of Horn & Hardart goodies at 8:30 A.M. from the subway station. "When she came in the door the children flew on her from every direction in their eagerness to begin the party. Everybody grabbed his food away from her, and each had his own party in his own corner. Food was going everywhere, up to the ceilings and down throats. The party was over at ten past nine."

Harold remains after school for remedial reading at primer level and, leaving him for a few minutes, on the way to the washroom I pass Mr. Rowby's room. Some tall boys—sixth grade? his own boys? Jefferson?—are hanging around the open door calling in to him. Rowby's got their friend inside.

—Wheee, Mr. Roowby, you a homosexual, Mr. Rooobey! Shi', man, when you go down that aisle you think you so hot, Mr. Rowby, that tail of you wave back and forth!

—I tell you, Rowby, if Waldon here, *he* take and smash you' butt, only Waldon don't go here no more.

—You such a faggot, Mr. Row-by, you a homosex-ual! you keepin that boy in there for nothin, you faggot, cause Waldon ain't around.

(Rowby was inside leaning over his table; he looked as though he would burst out crying or fall, but didn't close the door. He couldn't; they'd kick it in.)

—You got such a big ass, Mr. Row-by, you *better start doing something,* that ass of yours really spread now. I suppose you come in this morning, you gots on those sharp clothes, you *think* they hide your ass, but they don't. Mr. Rowby, you faggot!

Religion

Richard's church sends him to a summer camp sponsored by middle-class Negro members of a small community in Michigan. Asked what they'd think of the writing on third- to fourth-floor stair wall, he says, "Oh, those people wouldn't

61

even know one of those words on the wall. They are church people!"

Curtis brings in a cross at lunch hour he says he found somewhere.

VERNON. That's a Catholic cross.

CURTIS. It is not!

VERNON. It is so, they a body on it, it's Catholic.

(Others are ducking at Curtis's chest to see the cross, and imitate vomiting at the sight.)

RICHARD. Well, you got to have a cross in my church too! A big cross is at that door.

JOSIE (calls out). You get communion in that church, boy?

HAROLD. We do! We gets crackers and cherry pop!

RUBY. You been *confirmed* in that church?

RICHARD. I been everything. I been saved. If I gets bumped in the ass by a cab, that cab driver just got to take one look at this card. (Shows card; card gives prescription, ending ". . . and must respect and speak well to members of our race (colored).") We got a lot of baptism too, but not like on 116th Street. I know they got complete diversion there. You got to wear a white gown to the floor for that.

JOSIE (hanging on to Leanore's chair in excitement). *I'm gonna get me that diversion,* my sisters had it. They look so beau-ti-ful in their gowns! The reverend hold you head so you don'ts drownd.
—In my church in the South, when the singing gets glorious, everyone faints!
—Oh, that's *Pentacostal* Church. Christian reform don't do that kinda thing.

VERNON. In my church everyone gets communion, but you gots to be eleven.

RUBY. When you eats the crackers, that's eatin up Baby Jesus.

VERNON. If you go to church every week, my preacher will send you to camp for two weeks. You gotta bring four T shirts and swimming trunks.

RICHARD. Well, I am a *Christian.* The Catholics prays to the idol Mary. But it ain't wrong to be a Catholic, if it's okay

62

for you. My preacher says I'm going to have salvation, and he musta *read my mind* cause that's just what I got in minds for myself. I go to Sunday School twice a week, and I learn about Adam and Eve—Adam and Eve was stark naked; and the second worst sin. But I forgets what that is. And that's why I gets to go to Michigan in the summer, with the light-skinned Negro people—they never lock doors in Michigan and no one steals nothing.

RUBY. That's nothing. I'm Baptist and we goes to Atlantic City, but I never heard of Michigan. We goes with light-skin people and we sing beautiful hymns that makes everyone smile.

Addicts

A drizzling day. Richard arrives half an hour late to school. During the night, addicts had stumbled onto a pile of broken plate glass on his street, then into his building to sleep. His father, the superintendent, had found the hall so full of blood at early dawn he'd gone to the police station about getting the addicts out.

RICHARD. The lieutenant told him, "Dial my private number. I'll send every man in the place out."

MONTY. They gets blood on the floor because they misses their bein, too.

RICHARD. They sleep on garbage buckets in the basement. My father tries to get 'em out with his Derringer; but sometimes they get so high they can't get off the piles.

REGGIE. But they can't help theirself. It's their life. They don't want to hurt no one, just theirselfs.

MONTY. You has to be so careful with that needle, and be sure you go in your bein, and carry a baby's nipple over the tube or you hurt someone.

REGGIE. They feel they in the snow—walking in tennis shoes in the snow. They feel like they in another world. I don't mind if I was an addict—they *warm* in winter.

RICHARD. The reverend at our church, he tried for years to he'p them, but he say he about ready to quit. They do be so greedy, the reverend had four chickens for Christmas for the poor, and the addicts come and eat them all.

RUBY.   Children must stay away from them, they kisses you in a funny way, they wants to expose you. They splits open some candy and fill it with gray powder. They wants you to get funny with them.

MONTY.   An addict always brings his equipment with him. Cover his needle with a *baby's nipple,* and he need a big black belt for his arm so he can set that needle right in his bein.

RICHARD.   They cut when they sees the cops. The cops swing up they billies; they poke to the addicts' chin.

VIRGIL.   Oh, there was an addic', and I was *so* scared. I had my mother's twenty dollars; I was going down to the store. He come up behind me and put a knife on me and say, "Don't turn aroun', *don't breathe.*" Sometimes I'm nutty, and I run away! And I was lucky. You gets it right *there.* (Shows on his back.)

Addiction is higher than anything in any book, Mrs. Weiss says. Relatives of school aides may be hooked; parents may be. "In junior high, children go on the needle. Children with their heads down in cafeteria, falling asleep in class. I know of a fifteen-year-old in Jefferson, sister of one of our kids, whose mother is on the needle and got the girl hooked—so she'd keep quiet."

Every doorway in the morning—men with brown paper bags and bottles. Addicts high, standing, leaning, staring. Not drinking. Fifteen in a block on the way to school. Signs in front of every building: "No Loitering, Order of Police." Three addicts are stripped naked at noon on a side street. The police horse off a square around them. Children watch on the way back from lunch as the cops go up each rectum with rubber gloves. ("They private places, they might hi' it.")

Eight bent over a burning ashcan a block down from school, warming gray hands. All night. Someone tips alcohol on the can; blue flame licks up for a moment.

A young addict puts his head in a cab:

ADDICT.   Gimme a dime, that's a' I wan', a dime. . . . Okay, then gi' a cigarette.

DRIVER.   Buddy, I just don't have it.

ADDICT.   Then fuck off.

MONTY.   They keeps moving, and stay together so the cops don't see. They take lights from the hallways; that's why they always so dark. It is *expensive!* A bag of reefers, that cost a buck! And they shares them in the hall.

JOSIE. You on'y needs blue pills now. The doctor sell them to you for a quarter.—In my block, Brother and Little John are addic'. Little John he's nineteen, he pretty and very light. Has processed hair.

REGGIE. A lady addic' in our block. I don't know how she have her life. She's an addic'; and she's a lady. There's *nothin* will stop an addic' that needs a fix. They'll cut a head off and mess around with the body. They *gots to do somethin* . . . they won't stop at nothin. But when they attacks you, you gotta fight back. *You gotta do somethin.* I'm gonna pick up detective work when I grow up. You get a Derringer. I'd have my Derringer here, right under my arm. I'd say, "Excuse me, you need a cigarette?" to the addic', and reach up and grab down my Derringer!

RICHARD. I go to my grandmother's building, she live on the top floor. I like that roof of hers, there's pigeons flyin, but addicts up there too! It's scary! I take my Pepsi bottle and break the top off. Then I'm safe.

VERNON. I always carry my broken bottle when I go out to someone's building. But they's no addicts in my building.

REGGIE. You jivin? 122 is full of addicts.

VERNON. Well, they *don't touch my grandmother.* No addict in our block'd touch my grandmother. They calls her Maw.

RICHARD. Hey, Mrs. Weiss, that a real diamond or glass?

MRS. WEISS. Hmmph . . . it is quite real.

RICHARD. You shouldn' wear that, some addict take and get it off you.

MRS. WEISS. He'd have to take my arm off to get that, Richard.

RICHARD. Well that's just what he's gonna do. He's gonna take off your arm if he needs that fix.

NOAH. My father was addic', but he went down to Florida, got hisself cured. No addic' can work, no addic' ever been known to work, except maybe when he were a small child.

REGGIE. You has to put on coconut butter to cover up

65

the marks cause you can' go round with those holes in you' arm, everyone'll know you.

MALCOLM. But you can't just *start* addict. First sniffin glue; you 'bout nine. Later you goes on reefers on the roof with older kids. My brother smokes reefers but he won't let me come up, he say he'll cut my ass.

—About ten hangs out on *my* block. My super keep them moving in our hall. We live on the first floor, my mom got a police lock on our door. But it's *scary*. They call in soft through the keyhole when my mom be out.

—*My* mother don't answer that door at night. She says Who's there? but don't open it. And she keeps that can of lye by the door.

—My mother too!

MALCOLM. Lye! But you suppose' to use that for the stuffed pipes.

—No, you got to keep that lye. But people do anything with it. A lady in my block, she threw lye in a man's face. He owed her nine dollars, and she needed that. He said, "You better not throw that, there's kids around here." But she didn't even hear that, she was too crazy for her money. Threw it at him and he starts to scream, "My eyes, my eyes!" And the ambulance come, and a lot of people was there. They took him away, I don't know where. But I know when he comes out of that hospital, he's gonna shot her.

2

Miss Lionni, the Guidance Teacher, dresses in gray from head to toe and delves on Monday. A voice of honey dipped in chocolate.

MISS LIONNI. And Curtis is—

VERNON. He's home. He stoled a transistor radio yesterday and the policeman come to his house, and his father whupped him.

MISS LIONNI. Mmm. Let's hope Curtis has learned his lesson; he's such an intelligent boy. (Very intimate voice) And how is Leanore? Lots better, I suppose?

(The answer which is expected is: "I'm glad to say that Leanore has been trying, although she has lapses.")

TEACHER. Leanore, how has your behavior been? . . . You don't know? Boys and girls, who can help Leanore remember what her part in class has been this week?

MALCOLM. She gives the teacher hard trouble, called her a white cracker!

CASSANDRA. For a while she were calm after Miss Bowser work on her case. Then she fall back into her old ways.

VIRGIL (homework monitor). Mean mouth. Never does home work.

TEACHER. Of course, Leanore can be very nice at times—

VERNON. Take her coat forty times a day and sashay. If she want something, just go up to the desk and help herself like a princess.

MISS LIONNI. I thought she was doing so splendidly.

TEACHER. It's true that lately she has been better—but no, not splendidly. Not splendidly at all.

MISS LIONNI (moves to door, fixing a kick pleat). Well, I'll be picking up Monty on Wednesday. . . . And I'm glad to hear that Leanore has been doing so much better this week!

LEANORE. Don't worry, I'd love to go back. Miss Bowser is a fine Negro teacher who knows what she's doing, not like this white thing. I can't stand sitting next to Vernon, he smells; and Harold's worse, in rags and there's so much nasty stuff running from his nose, and wheezing from that old asthma of his. I wish I were home in my house. No, I will not sit over there. You can pass out math books, but don't leave a book on my desk.

VIRGIL. You're gettin one.

LEANORE. Don't give me one. (Flings book, takes coat, walks around room starting conversations at every desk.)

TEACHER. Sit down.

LEANORE. Can't you see I'm borrowing this paper? Don't tell me to sit down.

Shreds a few papers, stalks out. Often is gone the rest of the day. Lately, however, she's been remaining in the building, in fourth-floor hall, where she stands in secluded spots watching sixth-graders pass and hoping someone will come out to get her. Sometimes Ferré puts her in the door and walks on. Or she may be found on the third floor doing the

67

Watusi with first-graders, or even in washrooms on other floors talking to tough sixth-graders who rather awe her. In the last case, she returns to the room after a while.

She pushes a classmate with one foot, kicks with the other, then picks him or her up a bit. Never pushes some of them too far. Harold may attack Iris, "Listen, Fatty, quit bumping into my desk." Leanore has egged Harold into this attack. Comes right in, as Iris bursts into tears, "Now listen, Iris, you're not fat; don't let Harold make you feel fat; you're a very large girl, a big girl, but you're just—well—*nice,* Iris honey, certainly not fat. Large, but not fat at all."

RICHARD. Boyyy, she always tries to get back in good with you!

LEANORE. And Harold, you're supposed to be doing that *whole* page; that's fifteen problems. Why don't you *get down to work* instead of hurting Iris?

HAROLD. She said for us to do up to Problem Ten.

LEANORE. Oh, I'm sorry, was it ten problems? I was mistaken; I'm sorry, Harold.

Some mothers come to PTA, not Leanore's.

JOSIE. There was a fight, and Leanore's mother gots to go to court to help the judge. That girl have many things on her mind. *I* don't see why you pick on her; Leanore *too high* for this school. Miss Caroline never going to come; she can't be bothered. She gets drunk.

Monty's Mother

A frightened waif. Frightened of her boy, of the teacher, of the school. Round, gray face. Finally took a chair parallel to my desk; just darted looks out of corner of her eye so I could not see her face.

She fears Monty being taken from her. Murmurs, "I know you going to tell me terrible things, but Monty worse at home—he screams so, and hit those babies. Or else he go outside and play; that house could burn down, miss, that why I didn't come before, and I gots to leave right away now. I don't dare leave him alone with those babies."

Most mothers say, "Well, he's going to learn to read." They can't really raise the child's expectations or hope—don't really know where to begin. Yet in some vague way will insist that education is valuable.

Suzanne's Mother

She comes in a clean housedress. A large woman who says little about herself but who cooks dinner and cleans the house before going to work at night on an assembly line in Brooklyn. A job she's lucky to have, no doubt, but she is the kind of person who would have gone farther with more education or would be a supervisor if she were white. Suzanne sat at her desk. Her mother didn't look at me or at her but told her off. "No, Suzanne, you are not sick, nor anxious, nor disturbed. You know it, I know it, your father knows it. Nor underfed, nor have family cares. You go to bed at nine, you eat breakfast before you leave that house in the morning. Nothing but one thing wrong with you since you started kindergarten: you are l-a-z-y. In this world you can expect less, not more. I been passed over for no diploma —*you're going to get one.*"

Suzanne was soon transferred out of my class, but before that, her work did take a sharp upturn.

Jason's Mother

Beautifully groomed. White gloves. No delusions about Jason. "That's him all over, telling stories." She wants him doing social studies on a fourth-grade level. He doesn't read on fourth-grade level, nor do the other children, so books haven't been issued. And there aren't any books, anyway. "Well, I don't understand. When I was in fourth grade, I read fourth grade." Doesn't agree that he can't read at grade level. Nevertheless, I do get Jason a book.[1]

Mrs. Hervine had a father visitor. She'd lost her bearings with a disruptive kid named Bert on Tuesday and slammed a ruler on his desk a few times. She went home expecting to be called in the next day. There is always a possible lawsuit.

At nine on Wednesday she was summoned to Mr. Saltz's

[1] The District Supervisor, Mrs. Hallowell, has been working a long time to bring books for every subject in the curriculum into each grade. If the children can't read fourth-grade social studies, she feels they should have the books in their hands to look at maps and pictures and be responsible for simple information on tests. She may get this reform next year. The reason there aren't any books now is that sixth grade is probably reading them. More are probably not ordered because of the blurring of actual as well as supposed reading levels that persists throughout the city schools.

office, where a man six feet three inches tall awaited her. His hands hung at his side, so large that the fingers seemed not to manipulate. Bass voice. "You Bert's teacher? You don't look old enough to be his teacher, you sure you're his teacher? I hear he's been fresh. You know what I want? I want you to pop him good in the mouth."

HERVINE. Well, of course Bert suffers from anxiety—

FATHER. Suffers from nothin. His tongue likes to waggle and he looks for a victim. Then he starts branchin out and poppin off. He forgets who he is. You ever forget who you is at home, boy?

BERT. No, sir.

FATHER. No sir is right. I ain't playin with you, boy. School callin up and sayin Bert got this and got that, and this and that been written about him—Bert's got lazy, that's all.

HERVINE. Well, Bert's very verbal; I suppose he has a lot to say and—

FATHER. This chil' has nothin to say. He don't verble at home. The only thing I want to hear about Bert is he's in school, learning. I wanta settle this one thing: Bert's got nothin I wanta hear and got nothin to say at school except what he is asked: is that right—what, boy? ("Yes, uh.") What? ("Yes, sir!")

———————

LEANORE. Gimme some homework. My mother insists I get homework. She is *very anxious* you assign me some.

RICHARD. Hey, catch the big downtown talk!

TEACHER. You didn't do yesterday's. Virgil will give you a homework page when you finish today's arithmetic. And please ask your mother to sign the homework.

LEANORE. My mother signs nothin. She's not gonna put her name to homework.

JOSIE. Virgil's not going to give her homework and she's not going to listen to Virgil anyway, only to you, teacher. Don't you know that about children?

(Harold is called on. He pokes around for right page and word. Leanore has been reseated in desk next to mine.)

70

LEANORE. Oh, just pet him a bit.

TEACHER. Harold is going to read. May he? Please? There are just ten minutes before lunch.

LEANORE. Oh, excuse me. Excuse me, Harold. (Moves clock so it faces her. Her things now occupy half my desk.)

(Two minutes pass.)

LEANORE (calls out). Hey, Josie! Let's not eat downstairs today; let's get a hamburger, okay? My mother's got cirrhosis; she's back in the hospital, so I got five dollars from my father for lunch and dinner today. He came over. My Aunt Pearl's takin care of us but she can't cook, so he gave her five dollars too.

(Gathering everything she owns, coat around shoulders.
Josie ducked down, hiding face.)

Josie, where are you? Listen, I've got to get down to that luncheonette before that stupid woman—

(Exits, talking.)

JOSIE (Noon). I won'ts be here this afternoon, teacher; it my mother's birthday, and I has to help twirl and put up pink and green crepe paper. She thirty-eight. Never had her own surprise party, so she goin to make herself one. Maybe I gots to make potato salad or maybe we're gonna order out; the lady upstairs do catering. My mother say she ain't gonna cook on her own birthday.

Teacher's lounge

BOWSER. Well, I'd like a minute to myself in this lounge. Let's get the puppets outa here. I want to come in and have a cigarette, and look at the *New York Times* of which I'm a very selective reader, and I want the damned puppets out of here.

MRS. MERCK. The children have come in to re-enact an incident of yesterday where there are many mixed feelings—

BOWSER. Who's the colored puppet? The family lawyer? Bet you give her some real souped-up liberal part.

MRS. MERCK. I don't think you understand the purpose of this guidance, Lucille. (Leaves.)

BOWSER. I want to light my fag. When I come in here, it's for myself. I don't want to see Janice Merck, her puppets, and her six degenerates. I don't like the pop eyes on those puppets. Perhaps in the hands of a competent psychiatrist . . . but Janice Merck doesn't know enough to come in out of the rain; she's too busy chasing that engineer around her apartment building. I'm starting a petition to get those puppets out of here.

MRS. WEISS

I know Mrs. Weiss best—she's Reading Improvement Teacher and comes in three times a week. She knows my children well, as they all did fourth grade last year too. Brings in rebus readers of fairy tales, which children love. She's an expert and says the primary grades are like being put on the rack. She dresses in themes—1932 with flounces, *War and Peace* with a cossack blouse—a period dresser. Gorgeous antique amber brooch and bracelets. Greta Garbo hats. The children are not sure about the oufits but love the flow of dramatic changes and hairdos. They try to rise to the occasion, all except Curtis, whose whine she perfectly imitates. "I've never seen such a kid. I asked him to carry Roger's books. Roger was carrying the blackboard. Most kids would love to be chosen. Curtis whimpers, 'No, I don't care, I don't wanta do that right now; my arm is sore. If I star carrying things, everybody'll say hey, help carry mine, and I might lose them and everything, and Roger doesn't even sit next to me, and what if I dropped them or something?' And he never listens. Oh, I can't stand the way he snivels.

"Three new insights on Rowby painted on the stair wall today." (She is wearing a canary yellow cape with frogging today, and lace stockings with butterflies.) "I was just checking with my fingers crossed—know what I mean? They must really keep poor Mr. Rodgers hopping with his bucket and Ajax—he's such a nice old man. They don't seem to evolve; they're just there. If you want what's current with the faculty and student body, don't miss the stair walls."

Miss Bowser has said, "Cool the mother of the Petit kid. I hear she has a knife." She tells how Miss Myles was beaten around the head and neck last week with a loaded purse by a mother carrying a baby in her arms.

Mrs. Weiss tells of a mother last term: "She was a psychopath and got in the building to attack a regularly assigned

72

teacher. 'You called my kid a thief, did you? . . . Well, *did you?*' She was beating the teacher on the face, the teacher calling 'Help! Help!' Three aides locked the teacher, to keep the mother off her, in the room. The teacher then told the principal (not Saltz but Billy Murphy last year) she was going to press charges. Murphy was a nice guy but desperate. He didn't want those negative entries on his record—too many pressing charges or quitting, you know? He said, 'If you do, I'll make a bad entry in your file. And well—you won't know what it will be. I'm sorry but I will.' Then he went further. He tried turning it around on her: 'Well, *did* you call the child a thief?' She started defending herself without realizing it. 'Well, Mr. Murphy, the child did take the purse and when I checked it the money was gone. What can I say?' Murphy said, 'And why was the purse unguarded on your desk?' Then he worked on the aides: 'How did the woman get in the building,' till finally everyone was on the defensive and shutting up. He did put the blocks to the mother: he told her he'd call the emergency police squad if she ever came back again. Oh no, she hasn't. 'None of it ever really happened.' But don't take on the mothers."

When Mr. Goff had Curtis, "His mother came up one afternoon after four notes home. She was puffing from the walk up. Curtis played around Ed's legs and behind his desk. The mother (she was ginned to the ears) kept dropping ond, drowsy glances on Curtis. 'Currie not bein guh'd?' she'd say once in a while. 'Now Currie, you goin be guh'd now,' and 'Well now, Currie, if you not guh'd, I don't want you in this room. Maybe you' teacher better take you out for a while, Currie. . . . I know I can't walk this four flights up here again. You be guh'd, now.' "

Curtis has been gone six days. He comes up to the room at noon the day he gets back, but only to eat his garlic potato chips in back where it's safer than eating them on the street. Other children enjoy the chats together at noon up in front of the room.

RICHARD. Listen, Curtis's mother threw him out. She sent *me* out for a small can of tuna fish yesterday. I come back with it, and inside she sayin and cryin, "You give back that five dollars, Currie!"

CURTIS. That's a lie, you couldn't hear my mother, why don't you get your involvements straight! Talk about your own mother, why don't you!

RICHARD. Oh, I could hear good! "Give me that five dollar, Currie!" Talkin to you in that hall. *"Please,* now, Currie!"

JOSIE. Whenever I wants to hear anything, I just steps up close to the door.

RICHARD. Listen, she was *callin!* I knocks on that door with the tuna, she so drunk she forgot she sent me! She says, Get the aitch out of here!

CURTIS. Liars! Talk about your own house once in a while, big teeth! Why'n't you *talk about yourself?*

VERNON. No sir, I was a witness. That house so messed up inside, it's like coal! And they beat you with furniture, Curtis, don't tell *me* they don't. Your father bangs you, bangs Anita and James too!

In class, Curtis rolls and dangles baby things connected to rubber wires on his desk; he has on him comic books, pink lucite combination crayon and pencil sharpeners, masks, ghost and monster cards, a harmonica. So agile you can't tell what he's doing—slippery, hidden things. Knocks Reggie's book from the desk, Reggie dives after it and punches Harold; the spotlight goes on Reggie and Harold, Curtis appears to be reading a book on mushrooms. But what he is really doing is getting money from Reggie's inkwell. Reggie and Harold get punished. Leanore: "You keep thinking it's Reggie, it's *Curtis.* I could run this class better than you."

If he wants to paint, he'll come up not once but ten times in a morning, "Can I paint now?" sweet or whining, whichever wears you down fastest. "Well, why can't I start now? Then it could dry, then I could do the arithmetic later, then I'd be able to work on it the second time a lot better, so if I could just start on it now, please? And I'd rather be back there alone."

He can't stand reality, his own especially. Once I gave him a chance to paint at noon. He came up at 12:30 and for fifteen minutes quietly painted a Greek soldier—then forgot he didn't *have* to be there! I turned to get a teacup—when I looked around he was gone. In, out, in. "Well, if you don't want me to come in, it's okay with me; besides which I'm not sitting up there any more, I want a seat like Richard's. You saw that part about my tie fast enough but you didn't see nothing about Ernie. Ernie's teeth are rotten. Why's he so great, how come he can punch you, not me?" Richard, (inside): "She caught you, she didn't catch Ernie."

Curtis: "I ain't afraid of you and I'm not comin in tomorrow. And I'm not bringing a note." Once Mr. Ferré came by and said, "What's the problem?" "He won't obey, he won't come in, he won't take his seat." Ferré laughed and walked on. An afternoon can pass this way.

Curtis came in Monday, off Tuesday. Showed up Wednesday noon. Virgil was eating lunch in the room and called over, "I'd take him to Mr. Voorhis if I was you. The reason this school don't run right is that Mr. Saltz is too sweethearted. Can't mess with a kid even if he should." Harold called over, "If I was his mother I'd just tie him up and wet him down and beat him. He wouldn't play hooky no more."

"Now, just what's happening, Curtis?" said Mr. Saltz when we entered his office. Curtis began to giggle. He likes Mr. Saltz. So do I. Mr. Saltz could have an effect on the children. I said aside to Mr. Saltz, "He's a parasite in the class, an attention getter over any child. He's truant. He spends hours out in the hall. Can't we do something?"

Mr. Saltz talked with Curtis awhile. "Do you know what you're like, Curtis? You're like a bottle of cherry pop that has vinegar on the top of it. We know that it's sweet inside —far down inside—but to get to that sweet part we'd have to go through all that vinegar, and most people would give up because of the bad taste; they'd never get to the sweet part." As Mr. Saltz worked out the comparison Curtis listened, fascinated. Then Curtis talked about his reasons for not coming: "My brother tore my homework and I knew she'd be so mad, and then I got up late and my father was fussin and he has to sleep all day, and my sister was cryin, and anyway my teacher don't care if I come in or not." Mr. Saltz said with a smile, "Come on now, no more of that, Curtis. Listen here! Your teacher wants you here, and I want you here. That's why she brought you down here to me. Look at yourself, a handsome boy like you—why do you make up these things? You can go on your merits. We want you to learn. . . ." Finally, "So what do you say, Curtis? Let's go back to class." "I'd rather stay down here for a little while, can't I, Mr. Saltz?" "Well . . . all right for a *little* while; but mostly we want you in that classroom, Curtis." A little more talk, then Mr. Saltz said, "Now back to class you go. All right now, you promised. . . . No more nonsense. All right, *just this one time* I'm taking you up. You'll go back to school and up those stairs yourself from now on—okay?" Even on the stairs Curtis was still in the game. He loves to have anyone swing and bounce him up the stairs. Saltz would nudge or lead him up two steps by the

75

hand—he'd fall back one and look up giggling. "Oh now, come on, Curtis. You're doing very nicely; now come on. One more step, that's right; now *three* more, we've got two more flights to go . . . that's right, take things with a smile. And be good from now on."

DONALD DOWNEY

One morning a white boy is brought in: a transfer from another room. He is dirty, has sea-green eyes, and is strangely dressed. A stunned silence. Then cries break out. The boy and his older sister have been seen wandering and confused around the school for weeks. "The whi' cracker! I know him! Looka those shoes!"

Even ragamuffin Harold did a double take at the shoes. "I never *seen shoes that color!*" They were high-heeled, dull apricot color—the boy walked rigid-footed to keep them on. He wore a nylon shirt with two buttons, collar stuck in, no buttons on a winter coat held around him like a cape, pants falling to the hip (they are tied with a necktie or else he holds them up with one hand), and above the pants rim, shorts of a filthy orange-purple-beige plaid. Dirty, long red hair.

Couldn't spell his name and no one sent up records, so for two days I didn't know. He'd been beaten up the day he entered; had a black eye and neck bruises. He folded up in the seat beside my desk and sobbed quietly.

Mr. Ferré says that Donald's stepfather is Negro. He and his sister have been attacked and beaten many times since they entered the school.

Donald could make no friends in my room. "Haven't you ever been beaten up? Is this fair because he's white? What if Miss Bowser and I called each other white cracker and nigger?" Children gasp but won't give in. They call out "No, it's because he's dumb, he's a mess. Who wants to sit next to him!" "He smells like an old mop!" Only Jason will say, "It's because he's a different color, too." "What if you went to a school that had few Negro children? Would that be all right if they beat you?" Jason looks down and shrugs. A couple of children who are picked on all the time are now getting rather pleased to see Donald. He'll be taking their places for a while. Nobody would go to lunch with Donald the first day, then Vernon finally did because he can't stand tension.

Outside class, Donald and his sister still get beaten by sixth-graders who lie in wait for them on bad days. The sister is a stronger personality, fares better. Both children make acquaintances for a short time, usually second-graders who soon disappear. But if they get with an older group, it's never long before the sister gets crossed, calls out "Nigger," then "white cracker" and "nigger" fly back and forth, the Downeys disappear from school again. An assistant principal and one of the teachers were driving them six blocks home for two weeks. Beatings leveled off, then started again.

I was out with the flu for two days when Donald was too, and Mr. Ferré made some headway. "You must get along with this boy. He's very poor," Ferré told them, and "You also might make him hate his new little cousin." I got a dozen sentimental versions of this the next day.

Richard considered friendship, but Richard wears a blazer with "Columbia University" on it and insists on sharpness. Donald is a really weak and fearful child whose eyes fill with tears if you say a heading on a paper is wrong. Lately he comes in with dollar bills and becomes the man of the hour. Leanore: "He buys his friends. I got my four friends, I don't do that." Richard (laughing): "Sure, that's right, put your arm around him, Harold, maybe he'll give you another quarter."

On bad days, Donald is still singled out and gets protection from the office. He and his sister become monitors and are seen hurrying through the halls with tears drying on their cheeks, happy because they're in care of adults for the moment, waving slips of paper from Mr. Saltz to new teacher or assistant principal.

Donald comes in with old magazines and newspapers each day; or rather, they're not so much old as they are damp and curly, as if someone had started to throw out coffee grounds in them, then changed his mind. He shows a curled photograph (from the same place as the newspapers?) of people sitting around in a living room, laughing and eating lasagna. He says, "These are my friends." He wants to show pictures of a baby caught in a sewer pipe, a man drilling holes in his own forehead. At his desk he stores the papers, and sits chewing candy with wrappers of strange, unknown brands. But nothing really comforts Donald in his misery, in this room. He cries gently, works a little, swears (big vocabulary), then cries again. Or if he gets an opening to talk, slips into it. Holds it. Tightens the valve. Talks and talks, a teary, nonstop monotone.

Mrs. Hervine of the second-top exponent had him before me. "A natural scapegoat. Why has *she* done this to him? He's really a rather beautiful child. But this neglect. Ricky, the Puerto Rican kid in fifth grade, is white; he's clean, he's sharp, a little bit hippy; he doesn't get beaten. He has many friends. But Donald couldn't make it even with white kids. He has a weak personality."

He comes in buh-buhing with pomade fifth-graders have smeared on his hair, goes home weeping, talking, dribbling, swearing. Gone the next two days.

TEACHER. Well, maybe Donald doesn't like his clothes himself—did you ever think of that? Why pick on him? Everyone has to wear what his mother picks out. Suppose that Donald's mother—

CHILDREN. His mother's a white cracker too!

RICHARD. He lives by me, that house is real baaad.

RUBY. You go down his block; there's a lot of stuff comin out of the top of one window, look like a curtain rod and whole curtain.

IRIS. Yes, my mothah seen that too, say she don't know *how* that could happen.

Teachers bend over backward not to favor Donald. I don't leave the room with him or talk to him in the halls. Yet not one of the children except Vernon and Harold has given him a break. Harold plays hooky; Donald gets beaten; Donald disappears for two days. Then the mother turns up to accost some principal, with Donald cringing behind her skirt, a mulatto baby on her arm, straw hair in a rubber band, no teeth, wheezing: "Listen, this goddam school better start trying to do something about this son of mine."

LEANORE

She spends a morning cleaning her desk whenever my back's turned. Her head goes all the way into the desk with Kleenex; many trips up to the wastebasket with things she's throwing out, into the cabinet to get paste while I'm out in the hall chasing Curtis. She pastes a picture inside her desk top to give it a home atmosphere. "Please get your head out of there, Leanore. Will you, please?" Comes out banging it so hard, it sends shivers through William, Roger, and Monty. "Pardon meee?" Opens her book angrily.

HAROLD (reading). Is . . . th-th-is—

LEANORE (reads at double speed). Eagle befriends this

78

baby bear. Now Eagle has *two* pets. Is *this* the baby bear? *Mama Bear's baby bear?*

(Tears her math paper into one thousand pieces and throws the confetti over her shoulder.)

"I'm going to the washroom," she calls, and walks out. Returns in half an hour.

"No lunch, Leanore, until you finish the math paper."

"You're not keeping me from any lunch—my mother'd love to hear about that. You want a paper? Here, I'll give you a paper." (Tosses blank paper on desk.)

"Well, your mother hasn't answered any of three notes; I should see your mother. Straighten up this afternoon, or I go home with you."

She laughs: "Lady, you better not visit my mother! My mother doesn't want to be bothered."

All afternoon she has the boys on pins and needles. At two o'clock, drops on all fours like a graceful panther, glides halfway up the aisle, stops, calls up something through the rows in a velvety, strange language, so wild the children are shocked.

JOSIE.   Shame! I never thought I'd hear a child talk to a teacher like that! Don't you have no mind in your brain, Leanore? Girl, get up.

VERNON.   Listen girl, you think you're at home now? No wonder my mother don't want you in our house.

At three o'clock, as the children were lining up and William passed her desk, she snatched his folder of corrected papers and tore it in half. "All right, get your coat, here we go," I said to her, and dismissed the other children. She slipped outside the door and stood laughing. "You wouldn't dare."

"We'll see."

"I'm not going anywhere with you. Fifty times you've said, 'I'll visit your mother,' but I'm on to you."

She dashed away and down the stairs, laughing. I locked the room and in a few moments was following her out of the building. The air was sharp and cold, but boys played with bottles along the curbs or sat eating penny candy—one eating, two looking on. Leanore had appeared ahead, and trailed and shadowed me, always keeping about half a block ahead. She'd cross from one side of the street, cross back, calling insults, running. She didn't think I'd keep going. We reached her block. Adults talked in groups in the store fronts, and at the candy store on her corner, people of different ages stood in coats looking out.

I asked a woman, "Do you know where 153 is? I can't find the number." "No." People stood in the next building hallway—something going on inside. A little boy said, "I'm her brother; her mother's out." (She has no brother.)

At this point I heard my name suddenly called out— Leanore's voice! She appeared from somewhere in the dark. "Miss Burke, I'm here. Over here!" And she ducked around the fender of a Buick and into a building entrance.

The kid who'd said he was her brother sprinted in after Leanore, announcing me: "Leanore, your teacher's comin!" Then dashed back out and onto the street to tell others. I walked up three flights with Leanore hightailing it ahead of me.

When I knocked a few times, the door opened a crack. "Are you Leanore Hazle's mother?" A woman in plastic curlers peered out: "Yeah, what'd she do?"

It was freezing in the hall. "I'd like to talk to you about Leanore, about her behavior at school." The crack did not get any wider, and from within Leanore's voice screamed, "It's gonna be a lie!" "I wrote you a note," I continued, and with this the door opened. "Listen, miss, the reason I didn't come, I had to go to court. I been very sick. You wanta come in?"

The apartment was spotlessly clean, though dark. Plastic drapes, flowered linoleum, 27-inch television that Mrs. Hazle went to turn down. Big end tables with kewpie dolls and crowds of furniture. Beyond, a bedroom with double-decker bunks, Leanore stretching out on one and peeking around the door to see what would happen.

Mrs. Hazle fixed a few doilies, pulled shades even, and went out to turn down something bubbling in the kitchen. She re-entered with a baby that she set about diapering, with an appearance of listening while I said, "I've been meaning to come and talk to you about Leanore. She is a nice-looking child who comes to school beautifully groomed, she has a quick mind, shows leadership qualities. However—" The mother was not really listening. I turned to the trouble side: hooky playing, no classwork, language, tormenting of children, leaves seat or room when she pleases, drops small change all over the room—"*Stealing?*" the mother cut in sharply. "Oh, not exactly, it's more that—" "Well, boy, she better not be *stealing*, I'll tell you that much. That'd be just about the next thing I'd hear about that girl. Can't keep her cooped up here, but can't let her go down on that street any more; the neighbors want me to keep her in," said Mrs.

Hazle, delivering the last words with a gaze toward the bedroom that hinted at the long antisocial years of Leanore. Leanore was now calling from the bedroom, "Oh, Mama, don't believe this woman, she's a liar herself! Tried to take my lunch money, said it was Iris's, it was mine! She steals money, that's the kind of woman you're talking to, Mama!"

"Leanore answers me back, swears—" ("Dirty lie! This woman lies!") "—chews gum constantly, obeys no rules, starts fights all day." The longer the list grew, the less I felt that Mrs. Hazle and I took the same view of the list. It sounded like nothing but a list. Particularly when she now stood up, placed the baby on the floor, and walked to a cabinet just inside the kitchen door. She did call, "Go on, go on, I'm diggin you," back over her shoulder.

"I thought if the three of us could talk this over, we could discover a way to correct some of these things. She often leaves the building. I was about to report her truant two different times this semester—" ("Lie! Lie! Mama, don't listen, the only time I leave the room is when I have to get something, like if I have to borrow something in another room, Mama. This woman's been saying she's gonna come up here for three weeks and never came, so you can't believe her! If I do my homework she says it's wrong, that's why I don't do it!")

"Miss Bowser took her as a favor to me for four days and tells me that last year Leanore's behavior was so antisocial she was about to be expelled—" ("Mrs. Bowser's a big, fat black cow!") "—So that's what I've come to tell you, that this is possible again. I've warned Leanore that I might see you, and she always says you can't be bothered." The mother now came out of the kitchen carrying a strap with a buckle.

"I can't be bothered?" She walked into the bedroom. "You told this woman I can't be bothered?" Sounds of strapping began. "Oh, I'll tell you something! You've just about had what you're gonna get out of my life, baby! I'm not going to no court for no kid again!" (Strapping. Cries of "Mama!")

"There's no point in beating her, Mrs. Hazle. We must try to find out what is making her unhappy," I said, going to the door, but inside the strap arm was now working mechanically over Leanore who clung to the bed. The voice droned along with the arm, "Oh yes! I've got a couple of things going for myself now, no one's gonna ruin it! Oh no, no more trouble outa you, girl!" (Strap, strap!) "I've got me this new baby, life looks okay for a little while right now," (strap, strap) "and nothin's gonna go wrong again. No teacher's ever coming here again, no trouble, no judges;

81

I've had it from you! This woman don't want you swearing, chewing gum in your mouth, fighting, and that's what she don't want." (Strap, strap.) "—Shut your mouth—and when you go to that school do that, shut your mouth." (Strap. Pause.) "—Another thing, baby. No guy wants you if you don't have the diploma; they'll sweet-talk you, but they don't want you." (Strap, strap, strap! Nothing could now be heard in the room but the strap going in a burst of new energy, the cries, and the drone.)

"Mrs. Hazle—please!" But just as I spoke, not in answer to my voice but because of some loss of interest on her own part, the strap fell to her side. Staring at Leanore, she wound up, "And when Sidney comes Sunday, he can take you, lock, stock, and barrel, baby. I've got my own scene going; you ain't ruining it again. You can just go up the Hudson this time where they know how to handle kids like you. Where they take those radiator brushes. Remember? Louise there, and she is a forgotten child. No one gonna go to see her; Martin ain't; Ravelle ain't. I got me this baby. You and me are two different parties from now on. I spent a lotta time on you; now I lost interest in you, baby."

At this point an older sister walked in with, "Listen, Mama, I heard about some more things Leanore's been doing," and the mother got in a few more licks, saying, "Yes, Sidney can take you and your stuff in the bag Sunday. Sidney always tellin' me y'got bad blood, but it ain't my bad blood; it's his. And when Farrell comes Tuesday, he can take you, too," she added to the other daughter without looking around or ceasing to strap Leanore. "That bus goes from Forty-second Street right up the Hudson to that school" (strap) "and there's plenty of room."

Here I said goodbye and walked out. The strap stopped, but sobbing still came through the door. I stood in the corridor for a moment. No other sound. Then water began running in the kitchen.

Leanore was very quiet in class the next day but at noon brushed past my desk to snicker and drop a few words stranger than anything in the visit had been: "I never thought you'd come there."

Some Patterns

JASON

Kept at home, they call him chicken. Scared of kids. A tattletale. The only kid in the room who goes home at three, changes his school clothes, plays a little, starts homework. The social studies book goes home every night. He eats dinner with a family, goes to bed at nine. In the Harlem milieu, he fantasies just getting out and down on the street. He is the hero of adventures and rescues: "Oh, there was a great big fire in my building last night. I ran to the corner, I called the fire department. I knew that television box was photographing me, but I had no worry; this was a right call!" (Cries through room of "Shi', man, there was no fire last night," etc.) "I ran back to the building! First I dashed in and saved two dogs!—" and so on. Like Donald Downey's, his stories always end on some moral of home training: "And my mother said, 'Now, Jason, you must wash all that smoke and soot from your hands and face.'

"I'm up on the roof flying my beautiful Japanese kite with my friend Walter, turn around, see three addicts; they runs towards us, they grabs. I say, 'Walter let's get out of here.' But they grabbed us, throw us in a storage bin right down on the third floor, slammed that door really tight. I say, 'Stay here, Walter, because when they come back if both of us gone, they'll know something's up.' I cut down to first floor fast. I go from door to door saying, 'There's addicts. Everybody wake up. Addicts,' and back up to third floor to save Walter. He says, 'Is it safe now?' I say, 'Ssshhh'—"

JOSIE

Eats quietly all day—little clandestine snacks in her desk. Calls out to anyone but doesn't give much information about herself unless to get something off her mind early in the morning. She may lean over Reggie's desk and whisper, "My big brother wents to reform school las' night." Too many investigators and case workers are around her house, and her family's so big, her brothers so scattered and far away in schools. She hides these things but can't really figure them out.

She feels chubby and too small. Goes into deep silences when Curtis says mean things like, "Why don't you stand still? Somethin' so pukey about you." Tears running down her cheeks, she comes in from going to the washroom where sixth-graders had kicked her and said, "You wants to go pee, you better hurry up there, black girl." Evidently she has a shady, picked-on past with teachers in the school, too. There is one, a Mrs. Windhauser, first grade, who sometimes comes into the room. Josie goes and hides in a closet. She falls asleep in reading, ashamed she can't read, sometimes in math, and even on days when Mr. Wilcox, the science teacher, is to come in and Leanore, Josie's goddess, is walking around rousing people in the room so they'll ask intelligent questions. *"Please,* everybody, quiet in here, or he won't be allowed to come in." Flies to Josie's desk: *"Wake up,* simple cat, he's coming."

Josie tries so hard but is not learning to read. Sight vocabulary of six words: mother, father, brother, good, happy, baby. For about two weeks her mother puts up with the review work at night, then said, "Tell your teacher you don't got time for this. She can learn you to read in school." She works hard for a stretch, sharpening and laying out pencils, wetting a pencil tip, blowing on her hands. But sleep keeps coming down on her. Reading starts: every book seems to be open, even Roger's—then from across the room I see that Josie is sitting with her book closed, quiet as a little church mouse, not smiling, just sitting, staring into space, a foot swinging.

Mr. Goff had her but couldn't get interested. "There are thirteen in that family. She's probably up to midnight with TV, then sleeps with two or three babies, with noise and lights still on. . . ." He adds that she's not too bright, referring to her known I.Q. I tell him how she prepares dinner for four babies. Or instances of reasoning: I had asked her to call St. John the Divine and find out the time of Evensong. She got the exact information (she'd never made a phone call before) and then, knowing I was to go there with a friend, asked me for the friend's number, called the friend, relayed the information. And what of her moral fiber on some days? A reward in sight, she can make superhuman efforts. Nothing, not even Leanore, can tempt her. I told her that when Virgil and Malcolm had learned short vowel sounds, I was taking them to a track meet. "If you just learn some more sight words on your list, you can come too." In three days she added three more. Then something stopped ticking. "Josie, you can take home picture cards. Please, don't give up!" She looks toward, not out, the window. "Josie, what about the track meet?" But something about it is just too much. She puts her head down on the desk and chews. Second reading period in the afternoon, she slips the book off her desk and under her. "Josie, the track meet . . ." "No, I doesn't care if I goes or not. I didn' care so much 'bout goin downtown that day. I don' care 'bout learnin to read."

Josie's conduct pains Cassandra. One noon, just Cassie and Ruby are in the room.

CASSANDRA. Don' want to say names, but they's two girls in this class who is bad outside, Miss Buh'ke.

RUBY. Her and Leanore went in that store. Josie say, "Gimme a pound of ham, dollar eighty-nine a pound," and the lady slice it, and wrap it and they runs off, laughin! And her and Leanore grabs sweet potatoes and goes out, *laugh* and scream, throwin 'em at people's heads.

CASSANDRA. And when Leanore playin hooky, and we tuk that note to find out why. Leanore rah't in that laundromat doin the wash with her mothah. Mothah smokin a cigarette and handin over clo's to Leanore. Leanore in boys' pants, Miss Buh'ke. And her mothah say, "Tell that woman Leanore have a cold." Her mothah just lah'd and lah'd, Miss Buh'ke. And she say somethin else, too.

Once the PTA head, Mrs. Cavalling, looked in when Josie was standing with her coat on. "Josie Virginia! What is this going on in this room you're in?" "She won't take her coat off, so she may stand up till she does," I explained. "Oh ho, so that's how it is. No coats on in *this* school. I'll handle that coat on with Josie's mother tonight, that woman my first cousin," said Cavalling, and Josie got beaten and worked for a week. "Sure, that's one way," said Mrs. Weiss. "She hasn't got her wits working, there's too many people at home. The babies cry . . . she has no life, she's simply stifled. She doesn't really know why Cavalling turned up or why the beating, though."

HAROLD

Tattles and lies, violent asthmatic attacks. Mrs. Weiss, who knows the family well, says, "He is just a thing in his mother's house." He's one of eight children, five up here, three south. His fifth-grade sister is now a dime-store thief. "You dressed *so* stupid today, Blackie!" says Leanore, and where most kids in this color world would fight back ("Hey, did y'look at *yourself* this morning?" "That's all right, I may be black but you ain't white neither."), not Harold. "Don't make fun of no child's home, Leanore," is all he says, and sits with an arm across his chest all day to hide no button. Wears his outside coat even on warm days and has the answer ready: "I'm gonna have an asthma attack, Miss Burke, I was washing my father's Cadillac and I got caught in the rain." (He has no father.) Besides "black" and "Greasy Face" he's called something that is the worst: he swiped

Virgil's pen; a bloody fight ensued and Virgil said, "Keep your *purple black* self away from my desk." Most of the time Harold just sits silently, standing pools of tears in his eyes or neck stretched with asthma, whispering, "Please, I gotta sit by you." "Harold, you can't, that's Josie's desk; she's just out for a minute." "I was up all night. My mother's two babies was fussin and sick. My mother had to make a formula." I try to cheer him up by choosing a special library book for him, but he whispers, "I can't. If I take a book home, she'll beat me; she'll think I stoled it." "Well, I'll write you a note." "No, she won't read it! Please!" He begins to cry.

He has a mother who leans out of a window watching her daughter fight boys in the street. She yells, "Just kick 'im in the eyes, Sally!" Any trouble from the school with Harold or his sisters, the same mother beats them so they come in next day with open sores on their bodies. A compliment keeps Harold going for a little while. Then I will notice he's not in his seat—he's on his knees, going around the room picking up scraps and splinters from the floor, dusting and shoveling, using notebook cardboards. "Harold, stop it, sit down, open your book. You're very good at this but you're not a janitor; a janitor is paid to do that kind of sweeping. You're in school to study."

Harold is key monitor and says at noon, "We'll lock the kids out and visit, okay, teacher?" His idea of a visit is to dust and arrange the window sills. "Flowers would look nice here." Wants to tell things on other children at this time. "Richard's down there swearing, teacher. And he was greedy this noon and was takin all the desserts out of the lunch bags, and Miss Jonathan threw him out, and then he cursed her. Malcolm took the basketball this noon when it was my turn, and punched me, and I never did get my turn, teacher." Likes to hint at filthy stories about Mr. Goff. "You know what *happened*, teacher, a child's mother came in and said, 'You better not lift my baby's dress again.' Wasn't that terrible?" (He had Mr. Goff last year.) "No mother came; no mother said that, Harold. Don't say it again to me or anyone." You can't tell where the stories come from; he thinks of things not even on the stair walls. Looks around at me so innocently from his window dusting to murmur, "But she *did* come and say that terrible thing." Then he decides it's better to shut up than be thrown out. Just to be alone in this room with an adult is the happiest hour of the day for him.

Likes General Washington, British redcoats, dancing, Michigan, Bible songs. Teacher (we are doing *dig* and *dug*): "Small Eagle's mother dug camas roots yesterday. Today she is going to—?" Richard: "I don't dig school but I dig the *Frug*." Loves his Friday night cadet corps. "In my corps, the corps master says the nurses are running down, so everybody better come forward."

Richard's mother works in a factory in Brooklyn, and he volunteers for after-school chores. "No, I don't gotta be home; she leave early in the morning and don't come home till seven at night. That's why I talk so much in school. My mother is *moody!* She goes in that room and close the door, don't come out for two hours. But that's all right. Brother fixes hamburgers for us all, and we keep quiet so she can sleep. And she don't want me having children in the house at noon. If I forget myself, she take that key away from me. But she said when I have a problem, tell her. Brother and me divides the house together and let her sleep."

When I first began teaching here, Mr. Goff said, "Most of your class—seventh- and eighth-grade drop-outs, you know that?" Now I know this is probably true, except for two or three children, Richard one of these. His chances of life and education are provided by his mother, who puts money in the bank for him, and his church, which sends each child and many other parishioners out of Harlem in the summer. For weeks my children could not understand that dinosaurs did live on the earth. Richard did; he knows animals; he's been on a horse in Michigan. And many other things he understand because of this different world he enters in summer, where they wash hands and say grace before meals. "No one ever locks their door in Michigan. On Sunday, no hard playing, and be very kind all day on Sunday. I'm very shy the first few days I gets there, I say, 'No thank you' if they offers a second helping, but they say, 'You're welcome here.' After a few days, I gets over it." Richard is strict about facts, wants me to keep straight on how things really are. "I don't want to sound on Donald. You think you *know* Donald, Miss Burke, but he's not so bad off as you think. Soon as you out of the room, he's a-bobbin and a-jivin."

He likes the color of Donald's eyes, and Donald's chubby sister. "Boy their eyes all be so green! I sure likes that little fat one." He pomades Donald's hair whenever it is in front

87

of him. Donald no longer resists, just goes on eating his jelly sandwich with quiet tears in his eyes. "Listen, this is nice grease, it's gonna fix his hair, keep ashes off his face, ward off colds." Others argue, "It ain't gonna work on that kind of hair. He oughta have his hair processed. You need a stocking to hold it down anyway; his hair's too long; it'll be ratty. You need heat." Richard (Applying pomade): "Listen, this is gonna make his hair *real*, give it a beautiful sheen that'll last forever."

RICHARD. Oh, kids really believe in Miss Bowser with that iron fist. She is *real*.

VERNON. I was gonna be expelled I was so bad, then she worked with me. I got that fist! And she know how to dig in and find them two soft places in your shoulder, get that bone between her fingers. It enough to cross your eyes.

MALCOLM. Oh, if I was gonna be expelled, I'd get it at home, boy. My mother'd scratch and bruise me.

REGGIE. Not *me*.

OTHERS. You jivin? Your father throw you out of that basement window last time.

REGGIE. He did not; that basement's on the street. Sometimes he give me a punch just to clear the air, that's all.

RICHARD. My mother told my father, "No one's gonna touch my child," so he went to Florida and she say it okay with her. They *split up* because he was whippin me with the ironing cord, that old plug.

MONTY. I be expelled, my mother'd *send me to my grave!*

JOSIE. I gets whupped with that cord. She really put a hurting on me. Or she take and cut a belt in strips so it go into any kind of place.

JASON. My mother just discipline me, talks to me. She says, "No physical punishment."
    —If I go down with the garbage and stay too long, she is really laying for me when I come up. When my sister stole from my mother's purse, my mother make her get naked, and tied her hands to the bed and give it to her *real* hard.
    —My mother beats me on the legs—says it's the best place cause your legs are soft.

88

—Gives me two licks if I eat the food she's saving for supper. I pretend to cry right away and she lets me off. My brother runs away when he gets his licking. If he runs under the bed, she pulls him out and then really gives it to him.

—If I tease the baby too much, she really put a hurting on me. If you jumps away, she give it to you more.

—When my father starts hitting, he don't never stop but goes straight through. Used to use a hanger, but when he hurt my eye, my mother said, "No more hangers. Too dangerous."

—My brother let my sister go out on the fire escape when he be at my house. She punched his stomach with her fist, so he'd remember.

—My mother says it hurts more hard when you are wet. If I lie or steal in the dime store, she throws me in the tub and hits me with a strap.

VERNON (to Roger). How bout you, Football Head?

ROGER (high voice). Y-y-yes! I am l-l-lazy! My mother says—

(He won't tell Vernon, but Vernon tells the others. "His mother punch holes in his skin and put salt in. And throws him in hot water in the tub.")

—If *I'm* lazy and don't do nothing around the house, she'll hit me all over with a broom, or else throw a big shoe at me. I covers my head.

—One summer night, I stayed out to ten-thirty. She waited at the door and said, "Whatcha doing comin in so late? You can't fix your own food." I got it with the curtain rod.

JOSIE. When my mother were little, *her* mother puts her head in the stove, made it real hot, when she were bad.

LEANORE. Nobody as tough as Miss Octavia. When my mother was little, Miss Octavia whupped her so hard, my mother still has the scars. But the only thing my mother says is, "I'll put a fan on your tan."

REGGIE

So high, he's going through the ceiling. Loves snow, rain, Derringers, convertibles, crises, 125th Street, his raw silk suit. In a middle-class home he'd probably be making space capsules and rockets. Gets high on new clothes or his own hipster memories of fights, quarrels, big nights.

REGGIE. Feel this shirt. How about this—pretty good, hey?

TEACHER. Yes! Did you get this done in the laundry, Reggie?

REGGIE. You kiddin? My aunt did this. Feel that starch. Listen, I gotta stay out of that Chinese laundry. I called that Chinese guy a yellow cracker, he takes out a knife and tries to stab me!

He is Jimmy Cagney on Friday nights. "I'm walking along, I feels good. I'm walking along, see; we're going to 125th Street, I feels good. I got my new boots on; I looks pretty good. There's an extra girl in the crowd. She isn't anything, but I don't have a girl friend; I might as well take her.

"Hundred Twenty-fifth Street. You stands. Sometimes if someone got some money, you get a Coke—lots of times you move around on different corners. . . . Mostly you just stands. Some guys have to be home early; they sorta ruin the crowd. But I gots this new fe-dora on. I'm wearin it back on my head, so I looks taller; got my boots on—I really look good! So I gotta take my girl friend home; she has to be home at nine, and then—I'm walking along; I'm with my friends; we're walking along—*what do we hear?* SHOTS! I says to my friend, heyyy listen man, what' ya hear? *P-kew!* . . . *P-kew!* . . . That's po-lice, man, I says, po-lice! We better watch it! I steps back, I jumps back.

(Now re-enacting) "I look what direction *those shots* (pulling shirt open with excitement). I gots these new boots on, see! I jumps! I *lashes* out! I seeing red, I, I, I, I . . ."

Girls at Noon.

RUBY. We gonna see my mother's baby, Friday; she in the Home.

JOSIE. Leanore, do you not got a new chil' in *your* home?

LEANORE. We do not. That's a baby belong to Mrs. Simms, she told my mother, "Listen, I got to go out for some cigarettes," and she didn't come back for two weeks. My mother said, "That's the longest pack of cigarettes I ever heard about." This case is pending. We're hard put to keep this child. It squawks. It keeps me a lot too busy, trying to keep this kid happy.

JOSIE. But weren't that a baby from the Protest' Home, you gets paid to keep?

LEANORE. Honey, my mother is ver-y *ang-ry* about that baby!

IRIS. My mother's new baby is nine inches tall. He goin to be fussin and buggin for a lonnng time.

RUBY. My aunt broughts home her baby, and Sharkey supposed to gets it clothes. She say, "Where is the clothes for this baby?" and he say, "There aren't any clothes." She were at Sydenham Hospital and that baby came home in a *cab* without a stitch of clothes, and it were *collld* out! My aunt say to him, "Sharkey, pick up a few things," and he say, *"There aren't any clothes."*

JOSIE. I ain't gettin married cause there's too many babies followin me now. My best friends those babies, but they follows you! They follows you up the hall and down the hall, and then they follows you outside.

CASSANDRA. When you having yourself a real pretty dream, they come right in the middle of it. Wake you up.

IRIS. My sister gots that baby now. She come sixteen and gots that baby. A *bad* baby; it cry and cry! My stepfather says he don't want no more babies around; there's enough babies. She gots to leave.

JOSIE. She gots herself married?

IRIS. She had to!

RUBY. My mean sister, she gone now; she married. We all gets along better since she gone. My mother says, she can just scream and fuss with her own man. But when my little sister go off her head, it get bad again. The doctor gives her special medicine. She sees puh'sons that ain't even here.

CASSANDRA. My grandmother don't want me gettin married. She say it just too sad. The men be drunk; they be courtin other ladies right after they choose you. He'll tuk a kiss; then he'll be courtin you. Then he'll leave you for another lady.

JOSIE. But if someone be saying to you, *where's your husband?*

CASSANDRA. Then I say, I don't got no husband.

JOSIE. But a lotta people goin to say to you, *"Where's your husband, miss?"*

CASSANDRA. My uncle, he's not really my uncle, he tuk and beat my aunt's head. And she ain't even married to him. He can't do that. When you be married, the man takes and fights you. But my aunt not married to him. My mother say

91

to him, "Estes, where that license? You show me that license if you think you can bang her like that." And he never show no license. And my mother say, *"Then don't tuk up with her."* But he come and bang her head on the wall! And the blood popped all over, and my mother had to puts a rag on her head. And he bangin her, and police come, and my two cousins from the South they just standin there; they never seen fightin like that down south. And the ambulance come.

LEANORE. Oh yeah? There's a lot of niggers fighting down south, too.

CASSANDRA. Your man can bang you, then he just tired of you; he tuk a new girl and leave you. And if you gets a baby it gots to go to the fost' home. That's when the kid ain't got no mother.

JOSIE. I don't know how a kid gets borned without a mother.

MALCOLM (arriving). My sister gots a baby last year, but she gettin married. My mother goin to make a big weddin for her.

JOSIE. Even if I don't know my arithmetic, I still ain't gettin married. The mens just wants to give you babies.

LEANORE. I'm gonna get moving. My aunt's gettin married; we're gonna live in a new house on Long Island. My mother says we can't get out of here too fast. It's easier to have grandkids than kids. I'm gonna adopt me some kids.

CASSANDRA. You mean you get you some fost' kids.

LEANORE. No, I'm gettin me the real thing, the kind you get papers on them. But not around here. I wouldn't live any place around here.

CASSANDRA. My aunt was so beautiful. And he just bang her, and blood goin all over. You was there, Iris, you remember, the po-lice? You saw 'em, those big po-lice. Well, that was for my aunt. And they had yellow hair.

CURTIS AND MISS MYLES

Curtis was chosen for three-day-a-week reading class after school. The teacher is Miss Myles. They could only take upper-grade children, there were so many drastic cases. Once signed up, you must go.

Half a dozen times he gets away with "reading class"

92

while playing outside all afternoon. Then, "Oh please, please, please, please, I can't stay today; let me make up the math at home tonight. Miss Myles gets so upset if I'm not on time; she says it disrupts the class, and I have to do the rhyming words first thing. We go right to work down there; we can't lose a minute. Oh please, don't make me late. . . ."

Miss Myles paused outside the classroom door during such a scene at three on Wednesday. ". . . and I have to do my initial consonants first thing; I promise I'll make up the arithmetic tonight, and then I have to hurry to get out that nice book about the snowman. All the children want to share it, but Miss Myles wants me readin it first; so please, please—" Miss Myles walked in saying, "Baby, that's goood!"

(To me) "Boy! Today is *not* a reading day. Yesterday he wasn't there. He hasn't been there since the second day. I've seen him exactly once in five weeks."

CURTIS. I don't come in to reading because I'm always being kept after school, Miss Myles, because I *have* to be, because I don't get my work done up here; and many times you think I'm absent I haven't been to school at all, Miss Myles; and last night I was afraid to come in because I didn't have a phonics notebook and you said no one come without the notebook.

MYLES. Coming in to reading tomorrow, Curtis?

CURTIS. And another time, Miss Myles, I did come in and *you* weren't there; you were absent; you weren't even there.

MYLES. Oh, wait a minute, w-a-i-t a m-i-n-u-t-e. Is that the day I was in the hall half an hour with Malcolm's mother?

CURTIS. Well, I don't know, but I looked in that class, then I had to leave—you weren't there; I had to go home and help my mother.

MYLES. You've got a big talent there, Curtis. Too bad you can't put that talent to work for reading instead of just for lying. You can't read a word. That's why you're in the pre-primer remedial class—you read preprimer, but you're supposed to read fifth grade!

CURTIS. Why do I have to go? Vernon didn't go, and he can't read either. I'm not going. And you weren't there that day.

MYLES. Quiet, Curtis!

CURTIS.   You weren't there! (Trying to slip out now.) Lemme have my coat. Lemme out of here.

MYLES.   Ohhh no, sonny. You're not leaving now.

CURTIS.   You black bitch, lemme out of here!

(A dash to the door, and he almost makes it. She grabs him by nape of the neck.)

MYLES.   Let's hear the rest of it, what you just said under your breath, repeat it.

CURTIS.   I'm not afraid of you; I'll say it.

MYLES.   Yes? Say it.

CURTIS.   I'll say it. Fu—ff—

(Her fist has come up against his mouth. He hisses *Fff*—like a cat.)

MYLES.   That's the last lie and last threat for a while, baby. (Keeps the fist against his mouth. Pushes him into a corner.) I'm paid eleven dollars a night to teach you to read, and you know what, baby? *I'm going to do it.* You're lazy. You thought it was going to be puppets and games; then you found out it was work, you couldn't take it. But you're going to do it. (He keeps muttering but the fist doesn't move.) Say it! No, come on! Say what you're going to say!

(He slips under her arm.)

CURTIS (loudly).   Miss Myles, that white cracker we got, Miss Myles! She wouldn't *let* me go down to reading last night; she said it didn't matter I went to your class or not; she wanted me *in here*. She was gonna punish me; she made me—

MYLES.   Ohhh no.

(Slaps him hard back into the corner. He doesn't get away again.)

Start telling the truth!

CURTIS (new low, dirty tone).   Oh, you think you're so smart; you're so great big in that fur coat; I'll cut that coat to slivers. My mother was gonna write a note the other day and tell you she don't want me reading; it's too late for me to be coming home.

MYLES.   Listen. This coat was bought with years of hard

94

work. You better learn to read, Curtis. Play hooky, stay out of school if you want, but don't you pretend you're down there, and forget the lying and sneaking. It's all going to change now, because if I have to be up here at three to get you, I will be. And I don't intend to be your enemy.

CURTIS. (starts to mutter again, with tears). Fuckin black—
(SMASH.)

MYLES.   Come on, little coward! Say it!

(For many minutes her fist doesn't leave his teeth. He stares at the fist, chokes, hisses *Ffff*, but the fist doesn't move.)

Come onnn, baby, say it! Let's hear that short vowel! Say it under your breath that way and hope I won't hear you!

(Ten minutes of this, then she sits him down at a desk and stares him eye to eye, keeping the fist there. He tries to put his head down; she brings it back up with the fist.)

MYLES.   No, you look at me. You can't read. You've got the odds against you in this world, don't you know that? You'll be dumped in a cruel world, and no one's going to help you much longer. No place for a kid who can't read. Only you're going to learn to read. See you at reading tomorrow.

"Yes, maybe he'll show tomorrow. Who knows?" she said later. "We got somewhere today; we got inside him, but now what? You can't do this with him in a class; take forty minutes a day and that's what it takes. Maybe starting four years ago—but I've seen him around four years. Pretty much the same each year. He has to know someone will follow him up; we can't have these phantom figures floating through the school system. . . . Too many teachers have come here trying to save his soul; no one's given him the crack that might save him. Well, I'd haunt Guidance if I were you. He has to be kept in a class. It's too late, but next year he won't even have you or me. He'll have—but we don't know, do we?" [2]

[2] On a later day, Miss Myles said, "Try these out on Curtis," and handed me a list from the Office of Suggested Disciplinary Measures for a disruptive child. Most items we skipped over: (1) Mark him down; (2) Warn him; (3) Change his seat. Some others: (4) Isolate him (Where? Are they thinking of the 1860 schoolhouse—the duncecap in the corner? Isolate Curtis?); (6) Send down for a principal (They don't come).

95

Mrs. Weiss: "Yes, Myles is great. It is instinctive with the Negro teacher to help you out. Or cut you out, some of them; but not Myles. In any case, they're the ones who *can* handle the upper grades. Negro kids don't try anything with a Negro teacher. She doesn't take it twice."

In the three months since school began, several teachers have quit. (The school had a 70 per cent opening list in June.) One was the first science teacher, a young woman in English tweeds and walking shoes and long brown hair, who entered a fourth grade to give a lesson on magnets. The children threw the magnets out the window, she left and was replaced after many weeks by Mr. Wilcox. Another was a girl with a face like a line drawing and somber eyes. She'd asked for a Harlem school but got a low fifth grade; her gentle personality began to suffer from the all-day attacks and senseless violence. The day before Halloween, she brought in whipped-cream cakes for a party. The kids blew the whipped cream through the centers of cakes, plastered it on walls, ceiling, each other. She went out to get rags and did the cleaning-up herself, but then nothing happened the rest of the morning. In fact, the room grew very quiet just at noon. When she went into the coatroom, she found the pockets of her cashmere coat had been defecated in, and left within that hour.

Teaching

PICTURES IN THE ROOM

A few at a time, prints that are large and clear. Most children can identify the President; a few, Mayor Wagner. Two or three may read captions or get the gist of a statement—"Johnson talks with reporters," "American planes in Vietnam." . . .

We added a few: (8) "I'll turn you over to an aide." Answer: "My mother knows all them aides." (9) "I'll *send* you to the principal." Answer: "Listen, Mr. Saltz is my friend; you're the one's got the idea he's gonna do anything to me, and anyway if he did, he'd have my mother in here." (10) "I'll smash you personally." Answer: "If you ever touch me, my father'll smash the whole side of your face, and black and blood'll come out together. My father tried to kill a guy on the street the other day. My father has a knife. Go visit him if you don't believe he does. And the guy had a blade, too."

They don't know from week to week (except Richard and Donald) who Martin Luther King is.[3] The only leader they are all sure of is Lucy Baines Johnson.

TESTS

Arithmetic test: the answer is 298. Answers on papers are 26,793; 81; anything. Children who are intelligent turn in these papers. Josie comes up with erased answers: "This is right; you marked it wrong. I wants you to fix up this paper."

The only way to give a test is put it up on the board several times: phonics, alphabet, arithmetic. They have known too much failure. They expect to achieve nothing. Even if only a heading is right, I mark this and give a separate grade. Sometimes the child is more willing to take the next test.

BOOKS

Excellent library. Mrs. Suslov has beautiful captions, displays, pictures of Negro children running in the wind. Art work of her own—a branch bending with berries and nuts, in a white painted vase. A mobile above the shelves, children in old-fashioned costume dancing. My children love to come to the library.

All the books we want in the room. The children take turns selecting ten or twelve books at a time. A child reports on a book; then others want to. Harder books I read aloud—reptiles, birds—magic, unknown worlds. Even if a child can't read but takes a book home, he gets a word here and there. He begins to look at himself in a new way.

DESTRUCTION OF BOOKS

He may take it home only if he's proved he cares for it. The major problem: arithmetic books and readers are written and colored in. Five hundred books are missing from the library at the end of a semester. The profile of George Washington (in a library book) has drips coming out of

---

[3] This might be the result of divided attitudes passed down by parents, but more, it is the lack of exposure to any kind of general information. They did not know who Malcolm X was. Even after weeks, Josie, if asked about Martin Luther King, says, "He a moobie star."

Washington's nose, a tongue drawn out in ink so he can lick them up.

CURRICULUM

There is a University of Chicago film on heat and snow—evaporation of water—then no follow-up. Why show it? No demand for quiet. A ten-minute period of relaxed attention, children asleep or dreaming.

In class, Mr. Wilcox tries to reinforce, but it's too late. It's time for the lesson on pulleys. The range he's to cover defeats him.

He is a Negro who is to go into industry next year. He is conscientious but already thinking about how soon he'll get out of here. He comes in taut and shaking from sixth grade. Brings first or second data material with him, never less. But no questions are asked; he can't stimulate the children and tries hard. The children dandle magnets; they faintly get something about 'tricity, but that's all.

RICHARD.   I was passin that class of Mr. Rowby's and they *sure* don't work in there! There was Mr. Wilcox, sitting, looking at his equipment. I said, "Why don't you teach 'em something?" He say, ' Do they look like I could teach 'em anything?" And those girls up on those desk, they *throwin* Gallo wine boxes around in there, and screamin, and shakin their dresses, having a laugggh!

TV. Current Events

Jason, TV authority, rushes in: "There was a Negro on TV last night on the Ed Sullivan show! Sammy Davis, Jr., is a Negro, and he was on TV. Ed Sullivan stepped back and said, "Ladies and gentlemen, just a minute: I have a Negro here tonight. . . ."

TEACHER.   I'm sure that's not how Ed Sullivan introduced him. The point is that he was Sammy Davis, Jr. Who else heard it?
    —Me, me! I heard it! When he started those jokes!
    —Yeah those jokes! I listened at that whole show!

TEACHER.   Well, what were the jokes?
    —I *heard* those jokes, saw that whole show!
    —I listened at *Johnson* last night!
    —Hey, me too!

TEACHER. What did President Johnson say?

—He said we're gonna buy a new state or somethin.

The same thing for all the TV shows that fill their lives:

MALCOLM. Listen, there was this guy on TV for science, he made all this smoke come out of some water.

VERNON. Hey no, a monster walked into this operating room on the Ben Casey Show.

JASON. *Not* the Ben Casey show, stupid, don't tell me. I never even go down Tuesday, just so I don't miss that show. I'm learning to be a doctor, I gotta get used to blood.
—Oh, I can't stand our television bein' gone.
—My mother say if that set of ours don' come back soon, we gone's get us a color TV. We got two sets in now, they *just don't come back*. My father say he think the store sold 'em. I don' care; I hope we do get color. It come on in red, white, and blue on that screen.
—We put ours in that 'pair shop too; the screen jumps so much. We better get back *one* of those sets because I misses the Saturday morning programs.

LEANORE (calls out). When my mother and I go to the Apollo Theater, even if we're late my mother gets what seat she wants. She just says, "Honey, would you move down a little? I want to talk to my friend." And boy if they don't move, my mother just gives them a little hard pat. Does not put up with nonsense.

(Seizes Donald's paper.)

This paper is *not in fourths.*

(He starts crying.)

She said to fold it in fourths. You call this fourths?

TEACHER. Please leave him alone.

LEANORE. This child doesn't belong in this class. You know what you oughta do, white boy; get that hair processed; it is too dull. If hair's not right, nothing is. I'm about fed up with my own hair, and I'm not having Mrs. Jarvis plait it tonight. I'll plait it myself.

TEACHER. Who's Mrs. Jarvis?

LEANORE. She's looking in on us while my mother's in jail. Mrs. Jarvis lives down the hall. My mother said to Mrs. Jarvis only yesterday, no it was Wednesday, "I'm gonna report about that Simms baby; it had magnets coming out

99

of it." My mother fears no one. She said to Mrs. Jarvis, "When I see a child with magnets, I don't wish to know the mother. That mother *used* to be my friend. Not now." No, I'm not doing the math now, I have to finish this water color; it needs a lot of yellow in here—it's better to do this first. The math I'll take home tonight; if I do it now, the numbers will all run together if I work in this cramped space.

TEACHER. Just finish the arithmetic now, Leanore.

LEANORE. No, I'm not gonna. (Later) My mother left *early* this morning, but she's comin back, don't worry. My father's coming Thursday; he makes $150 a week. The cops kicked in that living-room door. My mother sees that door, boy, there's really gonna be trouble.

(Speaks to me for the first time as a human being).

Well, I gotta go home tonight. My sister's retarded; there's no one to take care of my sister.

TEACHER. But aren't you staying with Mrs. Jarvis?

LEANORE. Mrs. Jarvis is just plaiting my hair. I told you that. She's down the hall; she calls in to us, but it's scarey at night, boy.

———

DONALD (depositing smeared, runny *Daily News* pictures of L.B.J. on desk). Teacher, my mother makes me bring these to school because she wants me to be the best in the school. Can I get you your tea, teacher? When it comes noon, can I get your lunch? My mother says cut out these pictures for your teacher, Donald, in case she cannot get them, and when I win a prize I'm gonna get ice skates and keep them in a box every night and she's gonna check. And my mother says wash your hands before you comes to the table, because she's gonna get a new dinette set soon now; and my mother says we got to have a big salad every day and roast beef, and chew up every mouthful very carefully. (Class discussed nutrition yesterday.) And she says I won't have to go to school forever, and anyway, pretty soon we're going out to Long Island where there's *good schools* and get that country air, boy, and you go out and cut down your own tree for your own beautiful fireplace, and my uncle lives out there, and he gave me this new mackinaw, and I'm his favorite; he was in the army."

Donald is now taking orders for greeting cards from teachers and principals. Knows half the faculty. Boxes of cards with sequins and ribbons: "To My Darling Mother on Mother's Day," quilted satin card: "To My Beloved on Her Birthday." Some cards are: "Even the Robins Are Chirping That You're Better" (Mr. Robin in a straw hat, Mrs. Robin in a bonnet with flowers, warbling over a window sill), "A Get-well Wish for You" (an arbor and winding lane, bordered with foxgloves, larkspur, roses, bird bath in white and gold). A masculine card shows setter dog and booklined study—pipe and slippers by a leather chair: "Now That Your Birthday's Here Again." When very dirty or carrying card money on him, Donald gets beat up oftener; so hoping for a talk, I again write the mother, listing eye infection (he seems to have pinkeye), colds, need to see a dentist, etc. Four days later he gives me a mucused return note, "Donald is in very good health, but sometimes he gets a cold in his mouth." His card dealer must say to him, "Now tell your teacher each card is different, son:"

DONALD. Each card is different, teacher, and when I sell a hundred boxes I gonna get my mother this beautiful drier, and it's gonna be pink, and everything's gonna be pink. My mother says maybe that whole back room will be pink. When I gets the pink drier, it comes in a box, and I'm gonna keep it there. And after we move to Long Island (Vernon: "He's always movin."), I'll have my own room and no one can come in, and after these two boxes, I'm gonna get my next prize for my uncle—he's in the army—and my Aunt Pauline. And I have a aunt with a farm upstate in New York, and it's so beautiful and you cuts down your own Christmas tree. And it's not like around here, boy. And my mother says she's gonna call me for dinner, and every night we gonna have dinner at the same time, and my mother can walk around the house in the drier while she dusts her new furniture, because we're gonna have all new things out on Long Island, it's not like around here. And my mother, she's gonna have dinner at the same time every night and she says I better watch out if I don't come to dinner when she calls, boy, she's only gonna call once. (Michael: "Mann! He sure can talk a lot.") And we gotta be so careful with that new dinette set, nobody, Jamie or Louise can put their leg up on it; that set may have to last a long time, and my mother says it's gotta be kept nice for all the people we're gonna have on Sunday, and my aunt will come and my uncle, and chocolate ice cream, and we're gonna have goood times. And first, she's gonna buy the pony on Long Island and then the cart, but I can't let no child use that cart cause she's gonna get it on time and they might sue you if they fall out and

101

gets hurt. And that television got to go off at ten o'clock and no other kids allowed in the house, and that cart be *locked up,* and when we moves to Long Island (Richard: "Mannn!") that pony and that cart gonna be the first thing on the program, but no other children can use them.

MISS JONATHAN

Lunchroom—two small rooms—typical public school. But no pigging. Miss Jonathan, the cook, is hated but they say, "At the new school they're gonna get rid of old Miss Jonathan. We're gettin a new cook and there's gonna be collard greens and custards with sliced bananas and fried chicken every day."

Miss Jonathan: "Quiet boy, or I toss you out."

"Listen, woman, I gotta eat."

"You don't eat in *my* dining room ever. Quit acting like a nigger."

She has plastic roses, one in a vase, on every table. Every table scrubbed and slicked. One noon, I sent down for a can opener to open sardines in my room.

"Can opener, I open *you.* I just tell her *no* utensil leaves this kitchen ever without Mary Jonathan with it."

"But it's for our teacher!"

"Listen, boy, I heard you the first time."

TEACHER. But did you get the other thing, some sugar for my tea? . . . What'd she say to that?

HAROLD. I would never tell you what she said.

VERNON. She let us eat four desserts though, *if* we eat up the other.

HAROLD. If we *don',* she hold your head down on the food till you eats it. She a mean-tongued woman.

("She sounds all right to me.")

———

Noon. Richard has been punished at home for telling the police captain where the numbers men are taking bets.

VERNON. And on the way back we see big Lillian again; she lost again on those numbers and she were maaad! (He does Lillian's kick-snap, kick-snap walk, neck thrust out.) Here's how she walk. She flipping! Kick, snap, kick, say to herself, *"If I don't get those numbers next week—That* make you maaaddd, place your number, they fixin those numbers!"

VERNON. You play that number on your doorway; that's good luck, especially 261—that comes up realll often. My mother say, "261 is a good number."

RICHARD. Sometimes I can hardly get in my building; everyone paying up Billy the Kid in there. He the numbers man on our block, the runner, and his pants hang down lowwww from all that money he collects.

VERNON. You don't plays on Sunday, though. Them men are very religious.

RICHARD. Runners have the prettiest suits! Billy has *every*thing! He has every pretty girl; and he's slickkk to those girls, even though they tries to get his dough. That Billy *slickkk*, y' dont catch the sparks jumpin off him for free. He has a pretty face; he's worth about a hundred million dollars.

VERNON. He takes bets on his blue pad, and he hold it. Everyone callin, shoutin out their number, and he sayin', "One at a time."

RICHARD. I ain't never again gonna tell the po-lice they're playing numbers in my building. When the numbers men heard that I did, they come after me! My mother says they could'a killed me if they got me.

REGGIE (lives in the same building). When the po-lice come, everybody run up to the fifth floor.

VERNON. But those police don't reallly wanta break it up; they just wants their share. That cop hang out in our hall cause it's warm, but that's how he in on the numbers.

REGGIE. When things gets bad, the lieutenant get wind of something; he get mad and say, "There's gonna be no more numbers." Then they starts bringin peoples in. They don't reallly wanta bring you in; they throws you out by nine in the morning.

LEANORE. Not nine in the morning, nine at night. It's too late to just bring any more people in. The reason they want their share, those cops don't get paid too much neither. That's why they shake you down. But they don't tell that lieutenant. The lieutenant would can 'em!

RICHARD. My mother says you'd think colored cops'd be

103

nicer than the white cops, but they *just about the same*. But we needs police. They protects you from the big kids that throw the rocks, make your eye go out.

VERNON. No one persons owns the numbers. And when you win, they comes on your street and tells you.

REGGIE. They do not, they gives out winners in the tavern now.

VERNON. That's a lie! They tells it on the streets, too!

MALCOLM. Listen, I was walkin, and a lady called "Hey, Markie!" And Markie, he's our runner, waiting down there by the ashcan for her. And her dollar float down and her list for the numbers, out it float right in front of *me*, and I'm in a buck.

REGGIE. They don't likes to take bets from little kids, though. You gots to bring a note.

RICHARD. I know people that won seven dollars. The least you can play is a nickel, but you *can* plays a lot more, too.

REGGIE. Listen, I'm walkin along; it's a nice bright day, and first I see a cop walkin along my way, toward me (swings a billy), and then what does he *both* see but a man walkin along with seven sweaters he stoled in Blumstein's! The cop, he stop him and he says, "Excuse me, what you got there?" "Oh, I just bought myself these seven sweaters." "Well *I'm* not so sure you bought those seven sweaters," say that cop, and that cop took three and walk one way, the men went on with the others, and now that cop got *himself* three sweaters!

VERNON. Those numbers okay when you win, though. If you gets yourself put off welfare cause you took yourself a side job, you plays the numbers. You *got* to, to pay the rent.

WILLIAM. In welfare they send you that yellow grits and horsemeat, but the horsemeat's too salty; *I'd* never eat that.

VIRGIL. Well, you puts that cheese on *fried eggs*. I'm on welfare, and I *like* that cheese they send.

RICHARD. There isn't anything wrong with being on welfare.

MALCOLM. Are you kidding me?

CURTIS. People on the welfare are too lazy to get up. You wanta know how to get welfare fast: go *real crazy* and make your house junky as you can; then you call the be-vestigator and they get you the money right away! Before you can say *chihuahua,* they gets the check ready for you up at 125th.

(Josie is silent.)

VIRGIL. Well, that's all right, though; it's no shame to be on welfare!

RICHARD (laughs). The only reason you're saying that is because you're on it.

VIRGIL. It's nothing to be shamed of.

REGGIE. Listen, Richard, *you're* on the welfare.

RICHARD. That's not true! My mother works in a factory in Brooklyn.

VERNON. If you too broke though, you call up at Channel Eleven and they'll send you a check, if you have to buy a house or a boat. If it's a 'mergency, they'll send you the money the next day. You call the Chase Manhattan Bank; they are your friends.

CURTIS. No, you go to *125th Street;* there's an emergency door at that welfare. You go right in there and they give you the money.

RUBY. What that money you get then, Curtis?

CURTIS. Two hundred dollars!

RUBY. To do what you wants with?

CURTIS. *That is right.* They sends you the medicine and other stuff, that two hundred dollars is for freedom. You can go to some nice stores with that two hundred dollars.

RICHARD. There's nothing cheaper than John's Bargain Store.

RUBY. I wants to get my Christmas present there, but my mother won't go there no more. Nothing holds up but their socks.

RUBY. I went out with that whole welfare check to get it cashed once. My mother watched me from the window but I was scared.

REGGIE. On welfare they sends you that old cheese and dried eggs. Those're hard to get used to.

(Imitates his reaction to dried eggs. Josie won't look nor will Curtis.)

105

MONTY. Well, that cheese is good to put in a rat trap. The rats can't get enough of that cheese!

REGGIE. No, the best is that kind with holes in it. They puts the holes in so the rat don't have a chance to eat so much.

MALCOLM. Jimmy's father, he's always drunk, and he steals the welfare food, like lard, to sell. He takes one of those great *big* cans, my mother says costs about two dollars, and sells it to get wine. But last week there wasn't any to sell, so he took Jimmy's graduation suit his teacher bought him because he's so smart and a good boy, and sold that. Jimmy told his mother, "You let him in once more, you ain't gonna see me again."

3

Truancy. The School

Cold weather; truancy high. "Why don't you come inside the nice warm building?" teachers say these mornings to the gangs of children who hang around the doors, kicking the doors to come in or on warmer days deciding not to come to school at all. No day is related to the one before, for them. Some children, shivering with no hats or galoshes, feet wet, do come in. Lateness jumps; 15 per cent of the school is late an average of half an hour every morning and noon. At the next district school, the principal orders no attendance taken before 9:15.[1]

Ernie Petit has been out many weeks. A loner like Curtis, but unlike him he stays out on the streets: children see him riding 125th Street buses, hanging on by his finger-tips, or roller skating in the afternoons. Ernie peddles newspapers until eleven or midnight, or fishes in the Hudson even in cold weather. He knows every kind of fish and bait. Meant to take just a few days off but couldn't come back. Has no friends in class except Curtis. He truly hates school.

[1]At nearby Crispus Attucks High School, most of the student body is not junior-high graduated, but "transferred" because of age. Of the high-school graduating class of 325 this year, 50 students received academic diplomas, the rest general diplomas. There are 300 latenesses, 500 absences a day at this school where 60 per cent read below sixth-grade level. The union delegate has asked that Attucks be closed.

Ernie is a pretty boy, utterly neglected, every tooth in his jaw rotten from penny candy and bubble gum; the rest of his earnings go into water guns, monster cards, fish-bait, and once he stuttered "I like the b-b-bow and a-a-arrow, too." He has the mother with the knife. Children say he runs with older boys, glue sniffers. He slips into school at noon to eat lunch with younger children who eat later, so he won't bump into classmates. Many truant children survive in this way. When things get hot, down to the next school a few blocks east to eat lunch. Many children depend on the school. Vernon says, "Some days when I have to wait in lunch line too long, my stomach goes round and round."

For weeks, Monty has been wearing tight outgrown shoes that make him cry. I would say to him, "Why don't you take them off in reading today? Nobody will care." "Can't get 'em on again, once they're off," he mutters angrily. When he cried an hour on Thursday, I sent him home with a pass. The children say, "Hey, Half-a-Head still absent? Got no shoes?"

I went to ask the PTA head, Mrs. Cavalling, about new shoes for Monty.

CAVALLING. That mother's on welfare. She should have got shoes for her child.

TEACHER. Well, she hasn't and he's out. I sent a note by another child; she did not answer.

CAVALLING. Well, dear, I don't know about this child. Who is this Mrs. Boyd, she a stout woman? No? rather *short?* Light brown? You say she's not light brown, not stout—well, I don't think I know who she is, this parent.

TEACHER. We must get shoes for him and get him back in school. He was coming through rain three days last week to get here, and no socks. He might get pneumonia. What do I fill out?

CAVALLING. Honeybunch, I never heard of this child's parent; if she helped on any of my committees, I'd certainly recollect her—not stout, you say?—we all work *hard* on those committees to get a school going in this community, dear, and this woman has never given one minute of time to my committee. PTA money has to go into phonographs for the new school. This woman better go to the Bureau of Attendance for shoes for this poor fatherless child. We can't have phonograph money going into shoes for no unknown mother's child.

Eddie's Bar and Restaurant. Faces of men peer out over dark red drapes at three in the afternoon. No job, no money. Not drinking. Heavy static smoke hangs over them.

Four men in a Packard, double-parked, doors open, at 9:00 A.M., drinking from bags. They watch kids go in to school, watch school let out.

White women in socks and high heels, coughing and hacking in the rainy dark weather in —— Park. Children sit on the benches. They have left home for the day, but unless an iron hand has directed them, many will not get to school. They talk to old men and to each other.

——th Street. In afternoon, the street is like a factory let out. Hundreds of people looking out of windows—three or four babies peer out of a single window. It is hard to comprehend that 1400 human beings live in this block. Seven or eight barrooms each block ("Two for one"), with the young men in fedoras sitting on pool tables inside. Basement grocery stores, from which people emerge to go up to the street, carrying small bundles of high-price food: a six-pack of beer, a half-loaf of bread, a TV dinner, coffee cake.

"The street hooks them," said Mrs. Weiss. "It's so much nothing it's a drug. I gave Andy in third grade a quarter to get the *Post* for me yesterday. He came back with change. There's a thousand reasons he would not come back. His brother's on the needle; he's from a family of ten; he's one of the forgotten ones. He came back, but the street will get him one day."

A fifth-grade child was pushed off a roof by an addict yesterday afternoon. No note of this in the papers. They didn't find the mother until 3:00 A.M. Children saw the child's body:

—That *bone* stick right up through his arm! He died *this afternoon.*

—Oh, I can't *stands* dead people.

—Would you look at *your own mother* in that coffin?

—I loves my mother; I loves her dearly, but I *couldn't.*

—Oh, I would! I'd stab myself and jump *right in that coffin* with my mother!

LEANORE. Listen, when my mother was in jail, I couldn't sleep, only when it got light. A man threw a lady outa the window in our building; her brains was all over the side-

108

walk. And police had to come with a mop and pail and clean it up. And I couldn't sleep, only when it got light.

(Later. At noon.)

LEANORE. When you go to the morgue, they pull out one drawer after another and say, "Is this your person?" (Shows children, using desk drawers.) They pull this drawer out. You look. You say, "No." They pull out the next drawer. "Is *this* your person?" You look again, you say, "No." Then when you do get your person, it costs a thousand dollars, because they gots to have pantses on, the law says; and because they fills up the person with sweet things to preserve them.

IRIS. My auntie, that my uncle banged on that wall, she died. We gots to go to the funeral tomorrow.

Dirty streets and weather. Snow piles up and melts, superintendents throw more junk out of buildings along the curbs. It mounts up. Noah, who goes into areaways to collect old bottles from garbage cans (the children despise him for this), comes in filthy every morning.

A substitute teaches Mrs. Hervine's room. In teachers' lounge, she says, "Well, this is Harlem for the month for me. Three days a month are enough when you're fifty-five years old." Yesterday at 2:30, she had a dose of something that's a common occurrence. The class was reading. Hearing a noise, she turned—a tall girl was staring at her, and chewing. "Jimmy Fox in this room?"

"No. Who sent you?"

"Listen, is *Jimmy Fox* in this room, I wants him."

"What grade are you in?" repeated the substitute teacher.

"Fus'," said the girl. Some snickers could be heard out in the hall.

"Jimmy Fox is not in this room. Please leave."

"That's a lie, woman. I wants him."

"Please leave."

"He a light-skinned boy, not so light as you but pretty light. Where is he?" With which she backed to the door, leaning out to tell another girl, "This woman's lyin, she say Jimmy Fox ain't in here." As other girls came around the door, the substitute pushed her out and locked the door. The children went on reading.

Assistant principals are taking over rooms. Mr. Voorhis of sixth grade is Acting Principal for a week. He's great, walks the halls all day. Breaks up fights and mobs in the washrooms, drags kids back to rooms. It's not a job for a human being. He looks in my room just before 3:00. "One suggestion: for the sake of the room's appearance, let's have sweaters removed." "You won't be able to get them off, Mr. Voorhis, the sweaters are security blankets." "Let's try. This little boy, take your sweater off." Reggie looks at him and laughs. He tries Virgil, who swears heartily. Then he gives up—but not on other things he's enforcing, such as dead quiet the first thing in the morning before lines may enter the building. He has teachers meeting and heading these lines—for the first time. He goes around checking that each room is teaching curriculum. He works closely with aides, severe ladies, some in old-fashioned galoshes and big sweaters, who think school should be quiet. When they're not around, you know it. The halls get wilder.

"Yes, Voorhis is wonderful. I hope he's higher up next year," Mrs. Weiss said. "But so was Ferré when he first came here. He had the children playing in the yard every noon; he put out a loudspeaker, taught them square dances, games in circles, took up his own lunch hour, worked himself to the bone, that young guy; I saw it. He was overworking. Then—what is it that happens? The assistant-principal exams? A certain mentality passes them, for memorizing questions, and it uses up two years. Meanwhile, the candidate adjusts himself downward until he can pass the exam. Ferré came here from a junior high. At first he was appalled. He'd say, 'Go to the office, get a pass; you don't walk the halls in this school.' He had never seen administrators drinking tea at all hours of the day. Then the first of May he sent down, 'Do you have any extra sugar?' It's all so contagious. The school is already running not on the lowest but a low level, and Ferré moved onto this level."

Voorhis tries putting martial music on the P.A. before lunch. The children brighten and straighten. Mr. Voorhis was a junior-high assistant principal last year, asked for a transfer to this elementary school—thinks elementary and prekindergarten is the level to crack in the schools now. He wants a peace corps in Harlem. As a Negro, he has some advantage. Is not from Harlem but moves around it a lot. He thinks what the children need above anything is a sense of quiet.

Still, he can't be everywhere, and fighting swamps the school. Every hall has a fight rolling; any time you look out, screeching, flailing arms, water shooting across the walls or around corners. The door falls open, water flies in. Reggie flies out with his dukes up, "I'll break it up!" and the next minute he's whirling in the machinery. They're Rowby's kids, and one steps up, a rather large boy: "Don't get in

110

on this, lady. Don't go callin Saltz or Rowby. Rowby knows we're out here. He let us out."

The Sixth Grade. Vengeance

These children are twelve, thirteen, and fourteen years old. They are overgrown and beginning to fill with rage. Children who are quiet, withdrawn, or in any way not tough aren't heard from much after they reach sixth grade. Sixth-grade boys write up the stair walls; signs go from weird and funny to hatred for teachers. Sixth grade forces its code downward on the smaller children. The code is vengeance, storing up grudges. A Negro teacher told a notorious sixth-grade boy, "Don't ask for it, Elmer, don't take on Miss Cavalling. A lot of people here would like to see you *kicked out*. She can fix you." He said, "Okay, I'll cool her. Next year, I'll come back and get her." (The same teacher said of her own daughter, in a sixth grade in another school, "I can't thrash her any more. I'm afraid of her; she can take me on now.")

Many girls in sixth grade grow brutalized. One afternoon, we passed the girls' washroom. My children broke ranks at the crazed peals of laughter rolling out. I went into the filthy place where eight girls hung in stalls, some writing on walls, others just screaming with laughter, kicking doors. I said, "How long have you been in here? What rooms are you in?" A couple left, the rest pulled up skirts in front of me, jumped into the stalls, "Well, what's you want, woman? You can't tell me come outa here; get outa here yourself." Sex, laugh, and hate signs are scrawled high and low, around a corner, on a ledge, bottom of the door, so no one whatever height or shape need miss reading them.

Reading and Other Things

The main trouble is attention. All day, "Are we goin to gym? Goin to gym?" but I can't get them to multiply. "Roger, three fours are—?" Iris: "Seventeen." Roger doesn't know that six comes after five and can't see it on the tens frame. A tens frame is a board of one hundred beads arranged in sets of ten. Only one in a room. They don't have their own.

We go through review tables of 2, 5, 10. Then we mix them up. "Let's go over them *once more* now, boys and girls. Then we'll take a small test to see what we know or don't know." Even as I say this, Vernon is shuffling his monster

cards of green men; Reggie is playing with guns that pop
out of his wrist watch; Curtis is loading a slingshot; Josie
is wearing plastic diving goggles; Leanore is drawing girls
with bouffant hairdos and dangle earrings on the first page
of her reader; Donald is licking some filthy food wrappers.
One or two children are watching the board. "In *two minutes*
the Rexographed tests are going to be passed out." The children go on playing.

Reading is a better subject, and most children improve
in memory of stories or children's books of birds and animals, read aloud. They like my reading aloud. When I pick
up a book we've read more than once, they know they'll be
called on to tell some of it later, and love calling out "Five
facts! Five facts!" to the first child who's called on, or "You
got to tell how it *happened,* first thing first."

RICHARD. *First,* Washington was born in Virginia, son of a
planter; second, father wanted him to go to school in England,
not enough money; third, married this widow woman with
two children.

(Children remind him: "She was very *plump.* Laughed
a lot.")

WILLIAM. Teacher, my mother was livin in the South when
Washington was President.

VERNON. You're crazy. She'd be eight-five years old now.

REGGIE. Washington could never tell a lie, and he shots
down a cherry tree.

RICHARD. I'm not finished. Country called on George to fight
the British. Our troops had to get up their own guns, and
Washington had to go out and beg food for them, they was so
starving. Shared his beautiful red cape with his men. And
there was a British warship, a redcoat surrendered his sword
to Washington. (Shows pictures of these things, finally a picture of Washington in the backwoods learning Indian songs
and dances, living with the Indians.) Washington dancing
up a storm with those Indians!

LEANORE

Leanore was in the Home a longer time than anyone at
first understands. She doesn't mind revealing her past to
Josie.

JOSIE. In Children's Village, you gots to wear a blue skirt

112

all the time, and gets a new mother and father for the whole time you be there. They be your own."

LEANORE. Listen, where I was I wore a blue skirt with one big pleat and two small pleats in back. A nice jacket, very short. No matter how you will, that jacket will not meet that skirt. On the back of your head this lovely blue hat with two streamers made of that black, bumpy ribbon. Blue socks or white, depending on the day, and those socks had to be in perfect condition.

Leanore is reading *Madeleine* furiously, to get a leaf up on the reading tree. *Madeleine* is a beautiful pink and gray book, written and illustrated by Ludwig Bemelmans. Madeleine's class of twelve little girls is crossing the Pont des Arts, Notre-Dame and the Ile de la Cité in the background.

LEANORE (reading). There they go with hats on and streamers, walking in rows of two across the Seine, and that sad-looking teacher of theirs, Miss Clavell. Each wearing her blue uniform, white collar and cuffs, in rows of two.

EVERYONE. Leanore, your sister! At the DOOR!

(Leanore stands, walks to the door with *Madeleine* closed on a finger. Stares at the retarded sister. Returns.)

LEANORE. That's not my sister. (Reading) Yes, that special teacher walking behind, veil over her head. Now they enter the dormitory—oh yes, I see. Those sheets are white as snow. Will be changed every Friday, just like they were in the Home.

TEACHER. Leanore, we're doing math now.

(No answer. *Madeleine* is removed from her desk.)

LEANORE. Hey. Put that book back.

TEACHER. Did you say that to me?

LEANORE. No.

TEACHER. I thought you said that to me.

Leanore dislikes Donald but is working with his bronze locks lately, whenever he is present. Usually he gives in after a while.

LEANORE (combing). You should see the wave I'm getting. This hair is so silky, I will say.

CASSANDRA. My mother can't hardly plait her hair; it just like white people's.

113

RICHARD (moves over from his seat). Let me comb it.

LEANORE. Get out of here. I'm doing it like Ringo's.

RUBY. Let me try it. You knew I was waiting.

LEANORE. Girl, you'd ruin it.

RUBY. No, let me try something the other side.

TEACHER. You can't comb his hair any more because we're going to Assembly. Put the comb away.

LEANORE. Well, maybe I can do some more this afternoon.

(Replaces comb. Sprays herself with cologne on my desk.)

(Later, afternoon.)

LEANORE. Recently, I said to myself, "That woman's very delicate." Meaning a number of things. You find a very delicate way of saying certain things.

The main thing you should do, though, is something about that hair. A French twist would be beautiful—go to 125th Street, find yourself a nice parlor. . . . As to that child of your sister's: I'm glad you told me about that. On no account should the child have been left in that room with such intention. He shouldn't have been let out of bed. You've got to put him in that room *all* day by himself; if she'd left him there long enough, the child would never write on that silk wallpaper again and wouldn't touch nothing when he came out.

Leanore's main thing at this time is Claude, a new boy from the South. She turns him on and off. Bored during reading, she calls softly, "Hellooo, Down South! Hellooo!" until he turns around. Sitting behind him, she pushes a finger into his back. He freezes. "This is a stick-up. Give me everything you've got and don't call out."

Donald Downey disappears for a week. Returns in new coveralls. He stands outside the door and won't come in— at nine and at one.

LEANORE. I'll go outside and talk real nice to Donald. I'll get him in.

TEACHER. You'll get nothing in. (I don't wish her going out as more than once she's closed the door from outside, locking herself out.)

(Later.)

Well, what did you say to him?

LEANORE. Nothing. He's a jerk.

114

WILLIAM

Can't evaluate anything, yet has a quick temper, wants to get to the bottom of things fast. Jumpy speech out of the corner of his mouth, no space between words: "Well, you saw what those two guys did, didn't you, I can't stand that, that real black-eye guy, sixth grade, hogs the playground, well I seen him, I seen him on the playground, I know him, I seen him." "William, come on, that was last week." "Don't say that, miss, I know what I seen, I seen. I'm leaving, miss, you won't see me no more. Goodbye."

All love to make fun of him, even Richard.

RICHARD (On stairs). You can't read that wall, hey what're you doing there, boy.

WILLIAM. Well, I can read it!

RICHARD. Come on, boy, you can't read!
   (Papers are handed back. William's is never marked right or wrong; it is just checked. It is gibberish.)

WILLIAM. This is an important paper. Any Rexographed paper is important. Right into my folder; my work's always done on time; now I got nineteen papers in my folder.

MALCOLM. Yeah, but not a one of 'em's right.

WILLIAM. Yeah, but there's nineteen. They took all the figs out of the bags at lunch and threw 'em, and there wasn't enough anyway, and James pulled all the meat out of the sandwiches. Lonnie Long's dance parlor closing, moving outa the neighborhood. I asked downstairs but they wouldn't. Wouldn't give me sugar for her tea.—My folder's gone, it's gone!

   (He has jumped up, is hurrying around room.)

TEACHER. Now William, sit down, be calm.

WILLIAM. No, I'm leaving, no I'm really mad about that folder, I'm leaving and that's that.

VERNON

Sitting on a volcano. I look around at the sound of choking: he has his fingernail dug into Josie's lip in line; blood is coming from her nose. He must be calmed all the time. When he misses words in reading, he may fold up the rest of the day. Must be praised for any success. "Oh, Vernon, you read that with beautiful expression; you sounded just like Eagle, like a little boy calling. I would have thought you were my friend."

Other retarded readers withdraw during reading: Curtis and Roger draw, Josie sleeps. Vernon suffers through it. He keeps the book open and tries to follow. He sighs with pain, with relief when we close books.

A specialist takes Vernon and William out of the room on Tuesdays and Thursdays. The boys will make cotton snowmen and talk about them. Have they ever made a real snowman? What does cotton feel like? Snow? They may dictate to her their own stories about playing in snow, or things they've done this morning. Vernon has worked with her for two years. This year he's jumped from being a non-reader to a 1.2 reader. The children are selected by testing, interviews, and recommendation of the teacher. I gave her five names this year. She was pessimistic but put the names on a waiting list for testing. She said, "I could take out sixty per cent of the school."

Malcolm goes to special instruction, too. He is now a good 1.2 reader. A year ago he was like Roger, could not talk. Now he tells of every injustice, his face agonized as he gets the words out: "In that buildin Virgil lives in, that toilet's down the hall, that's *wrong;* they can't do like that."

VIRGIL. A MOTIVATED READER

Early in the term, Virgil was number one hooky player (and nonreader). I did not even meet him for the first three weeks. His parents didn't know about this, and we were able to get together. Next morning, the door opened and an aide dragged Virgil in by the collar, shoved him down an aisle, saying, "Start sturdy. Open that book. Never let me lay eyes on you again."

I don't know where the change began. Perhaps with making him homework monitor, since Virgil is very attentive to detail. He began trying to read soon after. I call on a child. Virgil, with finger and eye glued to the word, mutters it aloud just after his classmate reads it. And he is learning, in that way. By June, he may be one of the top readers.

116

Children don't know where he lives. He spends time between mother and grandmother. When he came back to school, he'd almost forgotten how to read.

His mother came in, the first night of his return, and said instantly, "I'm glad you brought that up. I know it was a long time, but he had *such* a bad cough."

TEACHER. But the truant officer said he met Ernie carrying groceries one day when he was absent.

MOTHER. Oh, maybe he meant he went down to the store for me once or twice . . . you can't call that *hooky*.

TEACHER. But he said you work all day.

MOTHER. Well, on my day off. Maybe he went down to the store for me on my day off and thought that was hooky.

The grandmother came in the next afternoon. She has been trying to get custody of him for months. "I told the court I'd come to the school. The only people who'd know anything about Ernie would be the school."

TEACHER. When he's been here, he's exhausted. His head is down on his desk.

GRANDMOTHER. When did you go to bed last night, Ernie? You say . . . eleven?

CURTIS. That's a lie, Ernie! We were out to midnight, sellin papers, remember?

ERNIE. Eight o'clock. I ain't playing wich you.

GRANDMOTHER. I'm hearing what I want to. Last summer he stayed with me, but it was too dull for him. Wanted back with his stepmother. She's a wino . . . When my son died, she knew there'd be some money; that was the only reason. Wanted her hands on the money. "Loves Ernie." You don't love a kid and let him run around wild. Doesn't feed him.

ERNIE. She feed me!

GRANDMOTHER. But you eat all day in school? What'd you have to eat there last night?

ERNIE (starts). Chicken, collard greens, mashed potatoes—

GRANDMOTHER. You sure of that?

117

He changes it to "Collard greens . . . red rice."

Other Children's Mothers

—Fatback is good with hominy but nicest with collard greens.

VERNON. Sweet 'tata pie. My mother can make it with her eyes closed. And red rice and blackeye peas. I love that crust. If I'm good, she cut off the crust and give it.

—Mine's makin 'tata salad today. We're goin to a dance this week end, she's takin *me*.

—My mother can make bumblebee salad.

—There's no such thing!

—I know what he means, that name on the can.

—Yes, she put it in with pickles and eggs; it go a long way.

MONTY. My mother made a cake for us yesterday, *so* good! I don't know how she thought it up.

> Hot peas and dynamite!
> I'm gonna get my supper tonight.

Leanore reads a copy of *Better Homes and Gardens* and starts a big discussion on "Which is more flavorful, ham with or without pineapple?" Next day she says, "We prepared it with pineapple. *Far* more flavorful." Six children get up and say they, too, had ham with pineapple last night —even Malcolm who's so light-skinned you can see him blush.

RICHARD. I didn't have no ham. I'd like to say I did, but I wouldn't story like everyone here. My mother don't have time to cook for us. Brother and me fixes somethin. But she take good care of us. Lays out my outfit every night. And when I get worryin about my life and everything she says, *"Let me do the worryin."*

(Later.)

CURTIS. My father's got a second wife, and I don't think my mother knows anything about it. I look at that picture on the television set and I think, "Who is she?"

TEACHER. But it's probably a picture taken a few years ago, of your mother when she was a teen-ager.

CURTIS. What does that mean? . . . I don't know. I don't think so. I think I'm gonna get my head fixed, like Monty.

I don't know what she wants with a person sometimes. Mostly, I guess she just wants you to go away.

My father ain't even workin no more. He hurt a guard at work, and he got fired and we're goin to court. My mother said, "If you ain't workin I ain't either," and quit her job.

(Angry, he goes to his seat. Others talk.)

—My mother says she ain't never gonna take off work again. She work in a toy factory and they ain't no business now; they calls her when they needs her. But she told my father she's not never gonna not have a job no more. She's always gonna have some kinda job outside.

—My mother don't work but my grandmother does, in Riverdale for the white ladies. Serves them their food and does some dustin.

—That's called a butler.

—She make fifty dollars and the lady give me her kid's old dresses.

RICHARD. My mother works in a factory where they make paper tablets, and her boss say he don't know how he do without her. Those tablets I come in with, those're irregulars; he gives 'em to her. All the other girls has to ask her before they gets to go to lunch.

—My mother's boss don't pay her except every second Thursday. She can't make it meet.

Ernie's mother is a presser, and when we made collages, he asked for a piece of gingham to take home. "She just wants to use her own cloth. Not the boss man's."

MALCOLM. My father don't work any more. But he was middleweight champion. He taught Floyd Patterson how to box.

Current Events

(Noon. Children eating near the bulletin board, discussing life at the White House. They don't get Mrs. Johnson.)

—Hey, who is she? What she doin to Johnson?

—It's his woman. She's tukkin a kiss.

—Oh yeah. That be nice.

—When rich people kiss their wifes, they kiss on the hand.

—Martin Luther King live in that house.

—That's a lie. The President lives there; his whole family does.

—Man, if I lived there, I'd have that whole house and

119

not let nobody in. And I wouldn't miss a day livin there.

—Lucy Baines Johnson is probably worth a billion thrillion dollars. Buy herself whatever she want.

JOSIE. I guess she could buy herself a river if she wanted.

—Bet she don't eat fatback.

—You kiddin? She eat just steaks every day. Everybody don't love her, though.

LEANORE. Listen, she gets herself a few nice things and you make fun of her. That's just sour grapes, like that fox she read us about.

When a new photograph of a famous person at home goes up, lately Mahalia Jackson, the children pass their whole hands over the picture, palms down, caressing it. They hate Harlem, but call it "around here." "I wish I was south with my people. There's space down there." "She don't want me around here in the summer, my mother don't. We're goin south, me and my brother." Leanore alone calls it "Harlem": "When it's real quiet in Harlem you know something's wrong. I was sitting on the stoop last summer, one o'clock in the morning, all of us having a *good* time, my mother and her friends. Then came a shooting next street. In about three minutes, that street cleared out."

(*Noon, in the lunchroom.*)

VERNON. Everyone loves Martin Luther King. He is for civil rights and that's all.

REGGIE. That is not all at all. And that's not even fair, she said she is sick of hearin *only* he is for civil rights. And never again does she want to hear he lives in the White House or is a famous singer. He is from Atlanta, Georgia. He's doing stuff in Mississippi.

RICHARD. He said to the judge, "Why don't you give the colored peoples a chance to vote? You wants to keep them for slaves?"

HAROLD. He is for freedom rights now.

Books We Are Now Reading

The Story of Turtles. The Story of Ancient Greece and Rome. Story of the Sun. Washington. Lear's Nonsense Verse. Rudyard Kipling's Jungle Stories. Some are chosen for pictures.

They're to look carefully at the pictures, even if they can't read. Leanore picked out "The Pied Piper of Hamelin"; she liked the illustrations by Kate Greenway: the children carrying chains of flowers, the Piper in "His queer long coat from heel to head,/Half of yellow and half of red"; the crippled boy in his drooping, blue velvet hat.

> All the little boys and girls,
> With rosy cheeks and flaxen curls,
> And sparkling eyes and teeth like pearls,
> Tripping and skipping, ran merrily after
> The wonderful music with shouting and
>   laughter.

Josie didn't like it, but sat down and counted the children, covering small groups with her left hand until she got to twenty. Then she covered the twenty with her elbow and added eight more with her right hand. She said, "Well, he's got a nice group there."

At the first reading of the "Pied Piper" poem, the language of Browning was too difficult and the room went wild, children jumping up in their seats and calling out when they heard about rats. I tried a week later with more success.

REGGIE (looking at costumes). Hey, wouldn't it be crazy if you met a kid dressed like that coming along Seventh Avenue?

TEACHER. Oh Reggie, come on.

REGGIE. No, I mean it.

RICHARD. They broke their promise to him, though; they had it comin.

TEACHER. They promised the piper a thousand guilders and gave him fifty. Wouldn't fifty be enough, if they gave him that big dinner they described?

CHILDREN. That don't count for nothin. They *promised*.

They like to hear short stories most, such as one of an English child who lives at the seashore. "That chil' gonna save that ship and that captain give him a million dollars!" They like to hear longer things such as *Black Beauty*, once I get to reading them, but never ask for them. No child says, "Please read *Black Beauty*." For nothing is ever finished in their lives; they don't expect a story to be finished.

121

A quiet lady who can read. Shy. Speaks only when she's called on (it is the Curtises who get attention in any class) but for all the trouble at home with her stepfather, manages to report on a book each Monday morning. Until Claude, she was the only recent Deep South in class.

"Pickles, the Fiah-House Cay-ht.

"Pickle, he were a *fiah*-house cay-ht. . . . Fiah-mens gonna git 'im a hel-mut; cause he tuk an' *save* that baby kitten! Cah-ied that kitten home. Lady called Miz Goodkin', she say, 'Pickles don' raht-ly b-*lonng* in a fiah-house—' "

Iris is very dark, her body beginning to develop, as tall as I. "Big Feet," they call her, and "Eyeball Shoes." Wears her birthday dress with bows in the back on Assembly days. Her size is her painful existence. A fight is boiling outside —Jefferson boys. "Shut up, I'll get my cousin." "Your cousin ain't nothin to me." "Okay, I'm ready for you. Come on. I'll knock the black off you." Iris comes back from the doorway into the room and stands trembling beside the blackboard. I go over to her: "What is the matter, honey?" She says to one side in her faint voice, "Miss Buh'ke, Jeff'son boys they talks to me at night, say they goan rake me some night." I cannot calm her. Her slender neck with its Adam's apple (her gesture of touching her long hand to her neck) and little head are trembling. "Miss Buh'ke, they say they goan, and I don't got a broken bottle with me tonight." She will not leave the building alone without Cassie any afternoon they stay after school.

In this neighborhood, little girls walk with their eyes down. Jefferson boys and sixth-graders torment them, go at even littler girls with fingers in a V stabbing at legs, and early in the term I had to help find and identify a boy who had "done something" to a first-grade child. The little girl was dissolved in whispers and tears, couldn't look to see which boy when we entered the sixth-grade room. The mother, a thin, poorly dressed woman, stood angrily in the doorway, hugging herself with arms that had big slash marks on them, her eyes darting around the room. "I'm lookin for the light-skin one that touch my baby. Get him, or."

CLAUDE

Wears suspenders. Went to a one-room country grade-school in Mississippi, where the high school was in the next room.

Can't remember the name of the town—something like Floradell, Mississippi.

CLAUDE. Ma'am, I gots all the *a*'s done. But they's some stuff left over.

CHILDREN. That south chil', he *sho* do talk southern.

VERNON. Down south they whup you; they *cane* you if you does no work.

CLAUDE. Sir?

TEACHER. Claude, dear, come up to the alphabet chart. What is the next letter after *a?*

CLAUDE. Ba-yuh. (Bear).

TEACHER. Children, just go to lunch.—Claude, didn't you do this kind of work in the southern school? What kind of work did you do there?

CLAUDE. We raise mewllls.

CHILDREN. Wha'?
—Listen, where the gym in that south school? I say what floor the *gym* be on?
—You have a junior high school?

JOSIE. Teacher, I be born in New York. Would you take *me* for a southern chil'?
—You raise animals in that school?

(Answer is, some kind of chicken and mules.)

—Listen, we don' got those animals up here; *this is New York.*

LEANORE. It's gonna be hard to teach that south boy; they don't get things down there. You won't find a southern child who brings any science up here.

TEACHER. What kind of science do you know, Leanore?

LEANORE. Listen, I *been* down south. Many a summer.

TEACHER. Please go to lunch. Now Claude, let's just look at this chart.

CLAUDE. Ma'am?

LEANORE. Teacher, *he don't know* how to say, "Pardon me," he's gotta say Ma'am and Sir; if you don't say Ma'am down there, Boom boom! "Pardon me" is just one of those ideas of yours.

123

VERNON. You gots to watch yourself on the street down there.

LEANORE. He will *not* be able to learn to say "Pardon me." You heard him yesterday. "Ma'aam? Ma'am?" But one thing they got down there. You put bad spirits that bother you in any kinda bottle and just pop the top back on it, and you'll be all right.

———————

Donald Downey hits on a good thing: helping the aides in the lunchroom, so that now he can arrange to be out of the room and with adults half the day. Running around the pans and steam makes him wild. Wants to go down early; gets back at 1:30 or 2:00. He is so busy, he forgets to eat lunch himself, dashing from counter to tables, polishing, scrubbing, putting chairs up and down, guarding entrances from first graders: "Now, children, stay out of here."

DONALD. And I got to go down *early,* those benches have to be up right away, because the little children have to hurry; then I got to make sure every child finishes, and those benches go right back up. Mr. Tobias says he might give me fifty cents or else three dollars, and Miss Jonathan says I pick up those milk cartons beautifully, and they don't know what they'd do without me, and Mr. Saltz says he was so pleased to hear about it, he likes to know about this kind of thing going on in this school.

MALCOLM. Listen, that old Miss Jonathan hold your head down in that food till you eat it. Don't never tell *her* you gonna puke about something. She'll hold down your head and just say, "Take a deep breath."

JOSIE. Makes me eats that raisin toast. But I don't likes the raisins and I tells my mother. She fixed Miss Jonathan. Tuesday, when my mother is here lookin for *you,* teacher, you not here so she wents took care of Miss Jonathan instead. Miss Jonathan don't bother me no more.

This comes as a surprise to me, that Josie's mother was up here "looking for" me. I had sent home a note recommending Josie for remedial reading class.

Then I remember something in lunchroom yesterday. Josie had always got the same justice from Miss Jonathan as other children. They can eat all they want. (Roger takes four bowls of soup. It must be all he gets to eat all day.) But throwing anything is forbidden. Children may talk in whispers. All assistant principals take lunchroom duty—none did at P.S. 200. Tall Miss Jonathan goes around the tables, checking

124

clean plates. Yesterday, Josie pointed to what she wanted from her place in line, and Miss Jonathan gave it to her without a word, looking away. They gave the next child in line the usual serving.

TEACHER. But what did your mother say to Miss Jonathan?

JOSIE. (smiles, like me remembering the little scene). Ah doan know. But she don' bother me no more.

Girls at Noon

CASSANDRA. High blood pressure an' can't do nothin. All he do is eat out of the refrigerator and go in my mother's puh'se. And do everything to make hisself young an puh'ty. Put Nox-ema on his face. My moth' say, "Henry, that ain't goan help you none, when anyone look at you. You ain' young no mo'; neither of us young any mo'. You got bald hair." And she pay those doctor bills, food bills. And he get up late. And sit around; then go out, he'p hisself to the good food in the refrigerator. Then go down to Smitty's and drink and drink, and come home really drunk, and start fussin, and cussin, and fuss with my mother, and cause her to lose her temper, and she say, "Leave my chil' alone. Never touch my chil'. Cassandra got an abscess tooth, don't you touch her." But he don't pay no mind to that. Bang me right in the jaw with his hand. Don't hit my sister cause she'll bang him right back.

RUBY. My stepfather's brother live on 122nd Street and don' like me. And he married to my aunt; he'll slap *her* and lie and lie. And he look for my aunt's puh'se. He can't wait till she go to sleep, and she change the puh'se forty different places, but he tiptoe and tiptoe until he find it. So I told her one time. I was there when she was asleep and he came to my door and say, "Listen: I don' want you drag your feet in here any more. Kill you if you do." Then he come to my house Sunday night and say, "Well, how come we ain' seen you for a while, Ruby." I say, "Cause *you* say don't drag my feet here any more." He got mad, but make like he was laughin, "Oh now, Ruby."

CASSANDRA. When my grandmother's husband died, my grandmother say to my mother, "Well, that's your father. We got to go to the burial now." And my mother say, "Well, I wouldn't have known I had no father!"

125

RUBY. When my aunt died in Chicago, my grandmother got all the nail polish and the pajamas. And my grandmother got some of the furniture. And the rest of it was stolen. My aunt, just thirty-five.

CASSANDRA. That high pressure, he's not supposed to do nothin; but he not ever that sick he can't keep goan in those drawers, find every bit of money. He's got himself strokes, and diagreetes. Never talk about anything but himself. When he drunk my sister laugh at him, but *she really mean that laugh.* And now she bringin her baby over, and drop it overnight with us. Her friends come in to see it and see her, and she don't even live with us. And she keep tukkin it up, and showin it. I say to my mother, "She act like that baby a doll, but it ain't a doll. She got to let that baby rest and air out." But she don't care when it scream, she just say, "Let it scream, that'll make it have a strong voice when it grow up."

RUBY. My mother said, "Let's go to the park." And I say no, it's too cold. My mother and sister be fat; don't tuk to the cold too much. My sister's white. But I don't care—I'm *proud* of my black.

—Once my mother live in a building where white people live. And she talk to a lot of white people, and they talk right back.

A Visit to the Guidance Office

At 10:30 Miss Merrill came for my relief period and waited with hair swinging, forefinger marking a place in a copy of *Catch-22*, drumming a bit impatiently on the door sill as she waited for a discipline problem to be settled in the room. I went down to Guidance to see where we could get with the most serious problems.

Many people were in the office. A clerk was telling a missing teacher over the telephone, "You better get in here tomorrow, Millie; he's mad." Mrs. Peliss was in her office. She is a supervisor I've never seen except at the cake sale, where she sat at a desk in a smock like teachers wore in the 1930's, doing something with pencil and pad—counting receipts? Mr. Saltz was in his office, holding a gang of boys who'd been brought in for stealing and smoking—four of these had broken in a sixth-grade room to get their report cards—and sending home for parents. Disruptive children who have been thrown out of rooms sat at tables with puppets. A teacher came through the door and hurried in toward

Miss Lionni, saying, "Look, I want to talk to you about Antoinette," but Lionni was in her corner, talking to a supervisor.

SUPERVISOR. Look, I want him out. He is ruining the second grade.

LIONNI. He can't be suspended. We've had quite a few suspensions this month. (Consults a card.) Jack was a very withdrawn boy—he *is* acting out, I must say.

SUPERVISOR. He's stronger than the teacher. He's turning her arm.

I reviewed things with Mr. Wembler, a new assistant principal:

DONALD

He has so many things going on all over the building, he's out all the time. He sells cards, works in the lunchroom; teachers invite him in to help with plants or retarded children. He's gone all the time.

LAMONT BOYD

He's not even in school now, no shoes.

His mother did go to the Bureau of Attendance but was ineligible to get him a new pair. When he's in school he's in excruciating pain. He sees spirits and can't describe them. Sucks his thumb violently. Guidance interviewed him but nothing more happened.

ERNIE PETIT

He needs to feel some concern on the part of the school authorities. Yesterday, he took children home to his mother's apartment at noon; they smoked cigarettes, sniffed glue, cooked pork chops and collard greens, set the curtains on fire, and cleared out leaving pools of water, to get back to school forty minutes late. I asked what they did about the water. "Nothing." Ernie's been in school a few days all semester. Now he's gone again.

CURTIS

He showed up in class last Tuesday with a stolen ten-dollar bill—it was the day after welfare checks. He got away. The children say his father beat him with a coat hanger that

127

night, opened the top of his eye. Can't we do something?

Mr. Wembler promised only to act on Monty though they already had a long file on him. "No findings. Can't or doesn't talk in interviews." "But what about the shoes? Can't we ask Mrs. Cavalling to make an exception?" "That's her department. You can do nothing but send out a truancy report on him—if you don't want to do that, what can we do?"

Ernie? Nothing if there's a custody struggle in the background. Curtis? Mr. Wembler agreed that a chronic truant child is usually one with deep problems. But only if a child has *already* cracked up can anything—from this office—be done about him. "Only demonstrably sick children. We are under too much pressure here. The truant is demonstrating out of school." The latest example of instant action from this office came when a fifth-grader threw himself on the floor in Assembly, screaming. Nothing less is the province of Guidance. "There's really no place to send the child unless he *is* screaming."

My relief hour had nearly ended, and there are no solutions within the school system at present. I walked out of the Guidance office past the pictures on the wall of Negro children in beautiful homes, happy children brushing teeth or playing with birds on a hill.

Guidance is doing its best here. It has to give priority to the lower grades. Children are mentally disturbed before they enter first grade. Second, teachers and substitutes too often simply dump children on Guidance. They cannot or will not, or are afraid to, handle disruptive but less disturbed children in rooms. So Guidance fritters itself away.

As I crossed the entrance hall and walked up the stairs, six of my children came tumbling down the stairs and right past me. "Just a min-ute! *Where is the pack of you going?*" I said from the top of the stairs. All six stopped in their tracks saying "Whaatt?" (They always do this.) Leanore, for the group: "Oh, we were just *looking for you!* Curtis came back; he's pulling in snow all over that room!"

We hurried back together. Miss Merrill was waiting at the door to leave, *Catch-22* closed at about page 200 on a slender finger. "Welll," she said, "some of the little girls were nice, but the boys were *not* nice today." Behind her, the room was sloshed with snow dripping from blackboards and the picture of Leontyne Price on the door. Children were yelling. A glance showed Curtis had merely come and gone.

I walked into the room—nothing had been done about the snow—and Miss Merrill said something to me from the door.

"I said, could I borrow a child for a monitor for a few

128

minutes." "A monitor?" "I mean—like *just for* a few minutes. Look, couldn't one of the kids take his coat—doesn't
someone have a coat on now—"

"Well—what do you mean—go out of the building?"

"Well, I just want to get some coffee . . . I thought a
child . . ."

"You mean go out on the street now, during school
hours?"

"No, I didn't mean that; I just meant to go get coffee—
lookit, forget it, all right?"

Absences and Substitutes

Mrs. Weiss: "The trouble with Guidance is under-
staff, overwork, and too many sick kids. We need skilled
psychiatric people, not just social workers and guidance people. One guidance teacher for six disturbed children per
room is totally unrealistic. No one, no one admits to the
number and condition of the children. But also it's not really
set up for the children.

"A few blocks from here there is a good school. It's eighty
years old, with multiple wings and stairs like ours; there
are hundreds of places for children to hide—and they never
do. Every child in the school is in his room all day. Low
truancy, zero lateness. Notes go home with aides at nine-
thirty if a child isn't there. The school reads on grade level.
The principal is a Negro woman, but that's not the point. She
has the same cross section of teachers as anywhere else.
They come from the same school board, same distribution of
assignments. But this level is what she demands. Her being a
Negro may play a part, though, because she *intends* her
school to produce children who can read. From nine to ten
o'clock the whole school is reading; ten to ten-thirty, phonics
and nothing else.

"So it runs that way because she runs it. A school can't
be left to what emanates from the Board—which isn't putting real thought into teaching these children, or we'd have
a licensed gym teacher giving them daily directed physical
training instead of so many O.T.P.'s. School would be a de-
sirable place to be. We'd have alphabet cards and tens
frames in the rooms."

On Wednesday afternoon, a child in the back of Mrs.
Hervine's room raised his hand to read. She didn't know
who he was. "But Albert, you'll have to go back to your
room. Who's your teacher?" "We don't got one; we got subs

129

every day and the one today slams chairs." He'd found himself a nice room—hers. She says, "I can't get him to leave. He slips in every day and I don't notice him; he sits in different places. He's in a third grade. He cries, then I let him stay. He says, 'I get sick to my stomach it's so nutty down there and she goes Eeeagh all day; I hates her voice!' No one's missed him yet."

At Assembly time yesterday, Ferré came by and put two fifth-grade boys in her room, which is quiet. "I can't take them to Assembly. They have a sub." Mrs. Hervine sat them in the back, but they disrupted the room for an hour, carved "fuck" on the desks, and one pulled out a six-inch switchblade when they were leaving and her back was turned. The children said, "You shoulda seen that *black* one he had."

There's so much knocking-about of children like this. Today, Freddy who's been in my room several weeks was found to have covered only two grades in the South. Slip-up in transfer records. Leanore: "Well, that's one child gone, I guess that's not gonna make you too unhappy. I wanted to say to him, but I'm not a fresh child, 'Why don't you make sure what room you're in?'"

The first day I was out with the flue, a young man substituted. Children: "He was really be-yewtiful, and he had jello hair. But he say he kick us in the ass and butt if we don't sit down and stop throwing stuff."

To Harold he said, "Where'd you get the clothes, kid, out of a ragbag?" At noon he told the children he was going out to plan a nice program for them, but never came back.

The second day was a fat middle-aged man who kept crossing himself and saying little prayers.

VERNON. Wanted us to stay in our seats.

CASSANDRA. Cross himself and keep saying his prayers, and call, "One, two three! Where should we all be?" And said he would give everyone a quatuh that was quiet. Give some quatuhs to the boys, and say he gonna get some more change at noon. But when he come back, still had only eight more quatuhs. I was quiet but he never did give me my quatuh. He was a *liah*, Miss Buh'ke.

The Children's World

The week that Ernie reached his twenty-fifth day out, I was going into the building at 12:20 and heard my name called. Across the street the other side of construction machinery was Ernie with some Jefferson boys!

130

I stood and waved to him across the street. He laughed. The boys around him had on dirty coats, unbuttoned, flying in the wind, arms slung around Ernie, who'd grown long hair and was wearing a silk jacket with "Dukes" on the sleeve. I called him. The friends punched him and yelled, "Hey do that, man, cross the street, tell 'uh off! C'mon, cross! Tell 'uh to drop dead!" He laughed, hiding his face but trying to drag away from them. They poked and stabbed one kid with a cigarette. They yelled "Chicken" a couple of times; then a cop was coming, so they shafted Ernie up under the armpits and dragged him away.

In the room, I for the first time asked them why. "Where does he go? Why is it better to be out there than in here?"

REGGIE. I used to go to the Ouija movies all day.

VERNON. We stays in the movies all day. When I goes to the movies, I don't eat.

WILLIAM. Go someone's house. Have some fun. Cut off the lights.

JASON. I go to Sixteenth Street (116th Street).

JOSIE. I wents up to Genevieve' house. Her mother be tukkin that baby down to the chil' clinic.

TEACHER. Then what did you do? Did you watch TV?

JOSIE. We didn't do nothin, jus' sat in the house. My sister used to play hooky all the time. But she eighteen now, out of school.

TEACHER. Well, what does she do now?

JOSIE. Nothin. She eighteen.

TEACHER. Yes, but what does she do?

JOSIE. Go see her friend sometime. Her friend work in a soda fount'.

TEACHER. Yes, but your sister. Does she have a job? What does *she* do?

JOSIE (getting angry). She don't do nothin. She help my mother.

WHAT DO YOU WANT TO BE
WHEN YOU GROW UP?

LEANORE. Nurse.

JOSIE. Nurse.

VERNON. I be army.

(Leanore calls out, "Teacher, when is World War
Four?")

RICHARD. Play the horn at the Apollo.

CLAUDE. Boy Scout.

REGGIE. Detective. I get a gun.

(Leanore: "If you have to commit suicide, you have to
have a gun.")

Marine. Detective. Detective. Work in a factory and draw
peoples. Private eye: peep in peepholes. Private eye. A judo
expert. Get married. I wanta be army. I wanta work in a
candy store. Policeman. FBI. Detective. Nurse. Detective.
Marine. Work in Sanitation Department. ("You gets fifty
dollars a week." "Shi', that ain't much.")

LEANORE. Only if I grow up to be anything but what I'm
supposed to be, she said *she* ain't supporting me. Like if I
grow up to be a drunk.

JOSIE (later). I don't think I grow up. Sometimes when my
big sister start messin with me, I wish I don'ts be here at all.

NOTHING

Mr. Goff: "Helps her mother do what? The Livingstons are
the notorious family in this neighborhood. Every two kids
have a different father. The mother's now on the fourteenth.
Have you ever met Gumdrop? That's the kid brother. Try
talking to him in the hall sometime. 'What's your name?'
'Gumdrop.' 'Oh, are you Josie's and Marty's brother?' 'Not
agonna tell you.' He said to Mrs. Hervine, 'Who is this
jerk, Josie, you know her?' He's six. That family has been
in Family Court so many times, the whole court knows them.
I think the last time, the court wanted to take Gumdrop
away and the mother blew such a scene in court: 'Take 'em
all! Take every child! Rip my heart out!' the judge suddenly
decided 'Children belong with the parents.' There is now a
home tutor for three of the children; the mother has a social
worker who helps her plan menus and teaches her home
management, such as putting garbage outside instead of in
the halls or letting it rot around the house. The two older

132

boys go to a psychiatrist. The total budget for the family is between $12,000 and $16,000 a year.

"Gumdrop is in O'Hare's room. She says he is sexually perverted, plays with himself all day and a few other things; tells her, 'Let me out, I gotta go mess in the toilet; I mess in my pants if you don't let me out, and she'll pin a diaper over m'pants.' He climbed out on a ledge of the third-floor washroom for forty minutes this week.—And that's the distance of some of these children from the plantation in 1965. They are where we left them. And all these one hundred years of slums, dejection and privation have only gone into producing her, putting her in this school."

Fighting: howling and tearing at each other in the halls. Raw emotion, all on the surface. Corridor fighting needles the children in the room. Anything does. "I went home for lunch and there wasn't no lunch, the gas was off. Virgil wouldn't let me in the lunch line, then he laid for me, beat me when I got back!" "That's all right, you hog all the food. I'll take y'on again if y'come on, come on!" "I ain't givin it back. It ain't yours." "I'll getcha, Bucky Blackie, I'll come back and getcha. I said you could have it yesterday, give it back, I didn't say today." "Hatchet Head! It ain't hardly yours, it's Vernon's and he stoled it." And almost every child leaves in the morning with something gnawing him. Vernon is eleven and has eight brothers and sisters. He is the oldest. Has been mean and picking fights for two days. Mrs. Weiss tells me his mother just returned from the hospital with a baby and at noon I say, "I hear you have a new baby brother, Vernon." He stares me straight in the eye, tears starting into his. *"I do not,"* he answers.

Mutual misery, mutual attack. Some cry all day; stay out in the hall crying, won't come in and can't tell you why. Malcolm: "Teacher, Reggie's hurtin on Donald." Donald (hastily, scared): "No he isn't, teacher."

I put a problem on the board—a rather long one—turn around, and two children are bleeding, three are on top of them, fingers stabbing at eyes. The whole thing has been completely silent. Pieces of skin ripped off a cheek. A little girl is crying with her coat over her head.

Choking guttural noises outside—not loud. In the corridor a third-grade girl, low-slung, stocky, is slugging a fifth-grade boy. Her eyes are cloudy; she drives her fists at him, "Fuck off, buddy," but he gets her head and beats it against the wall. My kids rush to the door behind me, Reggie's eyes gleaming. But for once it looks so deadly, most kids are scared. The boy and girl are ringed. A boy says, *"She turnin*

133

him on, let her get what he give her. She gotta learn to defend herself." The boy is socking her in the throat.

Rowby is not in his room. Desks are piled in the center; a picture of Grover Cleveland, scratched with ink, hangs below eye-level on a wall. The whole room sitting around on desks and ledges, coats on, talking. A boy walks across the room: "Hey, Hank, gimme a cigarette." No one notices that I walk in, use the telephone to call Saltz, and out.

There are teachers who have been attacked days after an incident with a kid. No one wants to break up the fights in halls. Mr. Pressman knows of sixth-grade boys who are laying for him. He gets in his car and drives off fast in the afternoon.

A new teacher in her early twenties, just back from her honeymoon in Honolulu, is waiting for the bus after a bad day. She looks at her purse, drawing a heavy sigh. Her hands tremble. She says, "I go home from here with pains in my legs and nausea. I can't cope with what I see all day. I try to tell my husband, and he says, 'They're ten years old, why can't you control them?' I called my mother last night, and she said, 'You're a college graduate with a degree, what's the problem?' I went to bed at eight-thirty last night; I didn't want to wake up this morning. No one will listen to me."

All day long through the wall, "One . . . two . . . three! Now stop it!" My children chorus "One . . . two . . . three!" A body is thrown against the wall . . . you know someone's been thrown out, for soon after a head pops in our door, vanishes. I stepped in the hall yesterday. A girl in a tight green sweater flung out of the room with a yelp, followed by a boy shoved out with his fists up, fighting.

ROWBY (comes out with line). Straighten that line! I mean it! I want a straight line *now,* or you don't go to lunch.

KID. I don't care about lunch. Listen, Rowby, I'm gettin mad, I don't care if the faggots in this line gets in line or not. I'm goin down to lunch. Y'can't pull this kind of crap, Rowby.

JEFFERSON

A pair at the bus stop: a handsome boy dressed Ivy League, tab-collar shirt, yellow slacks. The girl is drab, rather prominent teeth, an overflowing notebook, papers with limp edges falling out, enormous sweat socks. She listens enthralled as he rages first against a teacher, then a girl in his class.

BOY. Yeah, her and her *"Please* don't come in here again without English homework." I could cut her ass. And how be-yewtiful she talks. "My fa-ther. My bro-ther, Al-bert. My fa-ther. My bro-ther." Oh *Jesus,* her and her father, her bro-ther, Al-bert, *Jesus.* Makes you sick to your stomach.

And *her, Audrey,* know what *she* pulled today in Science? God! I swear to God, there's no kid in the room that doesn't hate her. Her in those starched blouses, and her perfect homework all the time, always doing the outside reading, and her books in that case she carries with her initials on it, uuuggh! I can't even look at her. We go on Nutrition today. "What did everyone have for breakfast?" "Coffee." "Coffee and toast." You know how the kids are— "Coffee." "Coffee." Some phony had orange juice. Most of em coffee and toast. Then *she* gets up. Everyone in class turns around. "Miss Smith, I had orange juice, Canadian bacon, and then I had cwas-sant with a glass of milk." Cwas-sant! I swear to God that's what she said, *cwas-sant.* And she has a glass of milk with that cwas-sant.

(His voice has risen in his hatred of this other pupil.)

Her and her goddam cwas-sant! I wanta' put my fist down her f——ing throat!

GIRL. Shi', boy, you know what she had for breakfast? She had red rice, from last night.

The Children's World

Richard comes in late one morning with a fine German shepherd puppy. He says, "I'm afraid about having him at home; the rats might get him."

MONTY. You gotta put him up on the kitchen table. If you leave him alone, put a leash on him. Formica top table; they slips on the legs.

RICHARD. They jump pretty high, though. I hate leaving him alone. I don't know what to do.

—A rat bit my baby sister on the finger. My father's done everything: he sets traps, he beats them, but they tunnel through those walls.

—You got to kill them with orange poison. Traps dangerous, babies get their hands or feet in them. You puts the orange poison on the bread, they swells up and strangles.

—You gots to put the food away. My mother say our neighbor must like rats. She leave all that food around. Leave

135

a dish of corn and rice on the table, they play in it like nothing wrong.

—You leave food, that's just wasting money. Jump up on the table and eat through a forty-cent loaf of bread, right to the other end. Cost you a great expense, not puttin things away. Don't put your bread in a plastic breadbox; they go right through it. Get yourself a tin breadbox.

JASON.   Rats left feet marks across my birthday cake; it had blue flowers on it. My mother has to throw it out.

—My aunt put a roast in the oven and next day open that oven, and a rat popped right out at her. She screamed and screamed! She ran out of the room. Man, was that rat big!

—My mother don't leave one single food for rats; but even if she don't leave no food around, she still puts that orange powder around, up high so the baby don't get in it.

—No, you puts lye down, very thick aroun' the borders and thick on the floor, and the rat's stomach gets burnt up from that lye. A rat died from that lye. He this long and this fat! (Holding up hands a foot apart.)

—They eat right through wood and plaster, not tin. They's tunnels all through your walls. You need tin—if you can't get flat tin, stick tin can in there, beat 'em flat, till you get tin.

—My mother always plugging up that hole, but she don't know how to hammer it right. Sometimes at that hole I just waits until they comes out. My big brother, he got combat boots, he steps on 'em; if they little, I can kill them with the broom.

—The only good thing is, they don't like to come out in the daytime. They're more for the night. Love garbage, hate light. My mother leaves the hall light on. Never cut lights out when there's rats.

REGGIE.   I dare you to come in my basement, honey. Those dead and alive rats will keep you moving. I always carry a stick or a broken soda bottle. Hide that stick up my arm. Sometimes, in an emergency, I have to go down get the garbage buckets. I'm too scared to even think about it now.

> Your house is so classy,
> You got rats as big as Lassie.

> I went to your house for a piece of cheese.
> A rat jumped up and said, "Heggies, please."

VERNON.   They comes out from behind the refrigerator when

136

you puts the lights on, when you come in from the show. But don't scare me. I sleep in a top bunk.

(Others laugh: "That won't help anything; they climb right up some nights if they want to.")

JOSIE.   I don't want to hear about rats no more—I'm gettin scared!

—They likes the night. Don't come out in the day too much. If all the rats come out around up there, they'd be pushing people off the sidewalk, but they don't. They stay in till it's night.

VERNON.   Rats when they born they red, but when they gets old they long and *gray,* man. My father when he see a baby rat bein born, he say they keep comin and comin.

—Our landlord should live in my house just one day, just one day! But it's no good to bother him, he live out on Long Island and he don't like people to call him up there much.

—You can sue the landlord if the rats eat the baby; otherwise you can't.

VIRGIL.   No point in calling the super; half the time he's drunk. He's a bum, my father said.

—Our super's drunk most of the time, so he don't be sending up the steam. He singing spirituals on Sunday and sends his little kids down to the basement to fix the furnace and big flames leaps out.

—It's bad when he don't send up that steam. My two little sisters has asthma. My mother have to keep the oven on all day.

REGGIE.   Boy, my father ain't that bad, gets drunk but never more than once a month. If he get drunk he send me down to send up the steam. But always he send up the steam.

—Our super never once makes hot water.

—Yeah, us either.

—Those rats look at you! You better not curse them or look back. Don't never curse a rat right to him cause he'll take your clothes—go right into your closet and eat up everything.

—They give you blood poisoning, and their teeth has more germs than to kill an army.

—I'm afraid to go to sleep, they's rats. I'm afraid of the dark, and my room's way down the hall.

—Not me. My cat comes in my bed and saves me.

—You gets yourself a cat. If your cat kills a rat, put it in a newspaper and throw it out back, for the old mean cats to eat. No home cat is gonna truck with no dead thrown-out rat. Before you throw them out, you picks them up with the pliers because he's got every kind of germs on his teeth. And his tail's got germs too. You look out that back window sometime, it make you sick, there's so many cats eating old dead rats.

—Best way to do, always try to break their backs. If you gots combat boots that weigh more you can step on them. That breaks their backs too.

—If you're lucky they come out from the pipe and go right in the bathtub. My mother and me, once we saw eight of them. You hit them with the broom handle and the other person keeps filling the tub with scalding water, and you drown them. The other person keep on hitting with that broom.

—We're gonna move to Brooklyn to a new project where there's no rats.

—My aunt's movin' to Long Island so no rats can get at her baby. There's gonna be hardly any cars on the street. And everyone have their own garden.

—I'm movin' south where there's no rats, just snakes.

RICHARD. In Michigan, they got very friendly white rats. They never heard of nothing else.

—Rats and cockroaches go together. In my basement you don't see just rats and cats; you see billions of roaches, too.

JOSIE. Roaches are all right, they washes themselves in sand. But my mother won't let my brother play with them. You can get rid of roaches. But a fly's no good: a fly sits in a dog's mess and then rub its back and front feets together and sit on your food. A roach would never sit on your food.

NOAH. That's not true! Don't *never* eat grapes or nothing's been in your desk overnight. We had grapes, every cockroach in the neighborhood come sat over those grapes.—I walk into a lady's house and steps on some roaches. She say, "Don't do that. Let my people go."

CURTIS. Wouldn't you get mad if a rat touched your daughter's head? Wouldn't you kill every one you saw? We're gonna move to the project in Brooklyn. I don't know how, though. My mother's gotta get herself an operation. I guess my uncle's gonna help.

RICHARD. In Michigan, if you talk about rats, they think you from the outer limits. They country hicks. When first they seen my skin, they call me nigger baby; never seen something like me before. They call like this: "Nig-ger baby!

138

Nig-ger ba-by!" (He demonstrates, skipping in front of desks.) I was ashamed, but they didn't know.

Later Richard speaks of his dog again. The children advise him: "If he be that little, I keep that dog in bed with me. Then you can feel his heart on your heart."

(At Lunch. Noon.)

—My mother puts the hall light on to keep the rats away, and it makes a funny shadow in my room.

—I puts my coat and hat on the doorknob, and it looks like a person to me. I say to myself it ain't a person, but it don't help. I really be afraid in that room, but when my uncle comes it's okay.

JOSIE. What he do? You get outa bed?
—No, it's just okay.

REGGIE. Oh, I get plenty scared at night. I sleep with my sister Cookie; she's two. I say stay *very* close, except when she eats watermelon and pees in the bed. But if I was watchin a scary movie, I try to think of the cartoons till I go to sleep. I say to myself over and over, "Popeye, Popeye."

RICHARD. That pillow can fool anyone.
—I hangs my coat on the doorknob.
—I keeps mine on back of the chair and I see it walking toward me.

JASON. The worst thing is to leave your shoes on, or leave your shoes or galoshes out there; you think it's a rat.
—When I goes to sleep and I'm really scared from something, I keep saying, "Change the channel in your ear. Change the channel in your ear."
—I get most scared when I see "Night Walker" on television. I'm afraid all night, afraid they will get me.

CASSANDRA. When Pres'dent Kennedy died, a dead puh'son come and touch me. I say to my sister, "Did you touch me?" The puh'son stood in my room and I was scared.

RUBY. My grandmother in the South, she was buried over the hill. We went to the burial ground. And she come back to see me that night, right through the door. She said, "Come up here with me where it so beautiful." Told me, "Be good in school and never get married."
—When you dies, you comes back one of three ways if you mess around with girls or ladies: you come back as a tomcat, a girl, or a fruit.
—My father died, and when I go to sleep I hear his chair

139

rock and rock, the chair he sat in when he was here.

—I sleep with my brother, but I jump into bed first to get near the wall, so no one evil can get me. My brother and me puts a pillow between us. If a monster or something comes, he could grab that pillow, not us.

—If you have a cross near your bed, the devil won't come. But your spirit won't come back neither.

—Your evil friend will hang your coat up in the middle of the room and leave it there.

—When my baby sister died, she come back as an angel and smiled at me. Stood at the end of my bed. I wouldn't look at her, covered my head with the blanket. But she went on smilin at me.

Ruby starts to recount about her grandmother again. But I have come from the back of the room saying, "Children, let's talk of something else now. It's good to talk about these things with each other rather than keep them inside, and they're very frightening. But children, they are not true."

RUBY (tearful). Yes they are true, teacher. It's not true when you say, "That's not true." What I said about my grandmother, that were true.

Donald Downey comes in staggering under load of new magazines for his desk, taken from a doctor's office yesterday.

DONALD. I had to go away yesterday, teacher, because I had to go down to see the doctor about my private; it had some terrible infection—it was so big I couldn't hardly get it in my pants—and my mother said, "You're going to have to see the doctor, Donald, I don't like the look of this." (Children come up to the desk to listen.) So we go down, and my sister and the baby go too, and we go downtown; and first I has to wait in the waiting room, then the doctor comes in and says "Can I see your card?" and I don't have one. Then two nurses come and I sit down, and one takes my temperature and they checks my eyes and writes down; then I sees me two more nurses go past; then the doctor comes back with another doctor and a book, and the doctor says, "This is a very unusual case, Donald, your mother will have to give you special medicine every night," and the other doctor says, "I wanta examine both other children." Then we goes home and my mother pours out a lotta medicine and I has to take every bit of it, then I always goes in my robe and slippers into Jamie's room before I goes to bed. . . .

(A new picture of L.B.J. and Lucy Baines in dressing

gowns having a talk before bedtime has recently been shown and discussed in class.)

And we talks for a little bit before we goes to bed.

(Later)

Teacher, I got to be down there at noon, get all those chairs down for the small primary children; Mr. Tobias says, "Donald, you must be here at twelve on the head, or I won't be able to pay you," and he wants me to be very prompt and always on time. Then today I got to go right home because of the sickness; my mother don't want me on the loose with that infection, and my sister when she was there the doctor said, "Here's another case for us; this girl has an abscess in her ear," and then he looks at my tonsils and said, "I don't like the look of that tonsil." And Miss Jonathan says, "Now Donald, you come down here at twelve sharp at the end of the week or I can't give you that three dollars," and I'm gonna put that three dollars right with my card money. And my uncle gives me a dollar, and he says, "Now Donald, I'm paying you this dollar because I want you to be in charge of my shoes for a while; you can make yourself a little change." And I got to take care of keeping them shiny, and that edge on that shoe got to be shined perfect and the whole shoe beautiful, or my uncle wouldn't pay me. And Mr. Ferré says, "Well, I don't really want to buy any cards," but like if I sold ninety-eight boxes, he might buy that last two boxes to make it a hundred.

LEANORE. Boy, you'd think for all the three dollars and one dollars, he'd take that filthy coat of his to the cleaners. (Over her shoulder) Hey, Donald, do that, take the coat in to the cleaner. One-day service, Donald.

REGGIE. Oh, why don't you shut up?

VIRGIL. Whyn't you put your head in the one-day service?

REGGIE. Yeah?

(Leanore laughs.)

VIRGIL. No, I mean it.

REGGIE. Make me.

(He has come from Row 6 to Row 1 to stand before Virgil, thumbs stuck in front of his belt.)

Yeah?

141

CLAUDE (enters). Teacher, Jason sah'l (soil) this sleeve of mine. I gonna get whupped. I'se got to wash it off, but I get whupped.

MALCOLM. Listen, put it on the radiator and keep it moving around when it steam, before it make a smell; no one'll ever know it.

LEANORE. Have the cleaner sew some buttons on, Donald.

NOAH

A hick kid from the South, whose mother has more than once gone to North Carolina leaving him alone with three babies in the apartment. Anything might happen. He is going back south for Christmas, and Curtis also—that makes three journeys to the South in a month.

NOAH. I'se goin' south for Christmas time. My mother say it better down there, she don' know the like of it up here. I don' care much. She shifts the luggage down there; I go on the train with my baby brothers. Gets off at Greensville. Walk rah't out to colored town.

TEACHER. But is that very far?

NOAH. No, it out in the country, my grandmother's house. It's a rah't nice little walk, but I get there all rah't.

CURTIS (has dropped in for a day). My father gettin new alligator shoes and goin down to get my godbrother for Christmas; he's in jail there cause he stoled a transistor, but he's gettin out.

REGGIE. What's his name?

CURTIS. I forget; it's too hard to say.

VERNON. South Carolina, that's my part. My brother comin up alone.
—I was in Virginia, but they calls me and my brother nigger down there.

NOAH. Got to shift your stuff, so you don't got nothing with you if you a chil'; be free to look for your kin. Ever' time a man go through with soda, you say, "I'll have a san'wich, please, and a orange soda." And drink soda all night long on the train. It cost very expensive, but it really good when you gets there.
—When I goes south I don't eats for several days, I gets

142

so excited! You can run and run everywhere. And there's garter snakes, and my grandfather take me in his car. I go in the fields and in that car, I go and go!

CLAUDE. My mother's sister sick, so she goin there; she's gonna cah-hy my cousin back.

Some Efforts

Josie almost climbs into my lap: "Teacher, don't counts me absent this afternoon cause I gots to take care of my mother's babies. She goin with my sister to Mount Sinai— my sister takin those fits again!" Then the biggest thing of the week-end: "I can spell *mouse.*" She stands up, closes her eyes, reaches into her soul: "M . . . o . . ." (Pause. Opens eyes to see no children are listening.) "u . . . s . . . e." Someone had taught her this on the week-end. This was to please me.

"That's wonderful, Josie, now can you spell *Hhh-ouse?*" She doesn't know what is wanted. "Can you, Malcolm? Listen: *Hhh-ouse.*" He smiles, shakes his head.

New books for the 2.1-level readers have come up. There are many good books in use in this school. Sometimes we're lucky, as last semester with *Dan Frontier.* Oftener, a freak set arrives. The latest is about a kitten named Muffy, a child named Bonny who visits seashore or grandmother; Bonny's mother, in a dress that hits well below the calf, stands on a knoll with poppies and daisies blowing around her feet in nurses' shoes, cupping hand to lips, baby finger extended, calling "Bonnie! Bonnie!" (Josie: "Her dress is always blow-in.") Another book that flips out the children is copyright 1939, containing a mother whose skirt flounces out at the bottom like rose petals, and marcelled hair. She calls Father at the office, using a post telephone. He wears a double-breasted suit with wide lapels, and a snap brim hat. The post-man drives a car with a front cab and running board; the wheels are skinny and reach halfway up to the roof; the postman wears a cap with peak resting just above his eyes, held up by his ears. In the Bonny book, the dog's mouth hangs open, and on page 17 the dye in the print has slipped so his eye hangs to one side. Children: "Heyyy—look at page seventeen."

Needed: a book written from stories by the children of Harlem, beautifully illustrated, about a real child in Harlem who experiences some kind of success. Everyone agrees on this. But we still do not see such a basic reader in use in most schools.

Stories Aloud

A Czechoslovakian folk tale of a girl with petticoats who helps animals in the forest.

CHILDREN. Whatsa petticoat?

LEANORE. If you got a real beautiful dress and you're going to your grandmother's on Christmas Day, your skirt's out like this and it's realll pretty.

My sister in the Home in Washington's coming home before Christmas, boy, if my aunt has anything to do with it. My sister bites people in the shoulder, but wouldn't be so agitated if she was out in society once in a while. We're moving to Long Island, and teach her to eat in public.

(Later. Cleaning cabinet) I'm putting this paper all on the left side; if you went to this cabinet, you'd feel paper, wouldn't know where you were. Boy, whoever did this cabinet didn't have no mother. (Cleans; gathers scissors, paste, construction paper, has flown back to her seat and made two Christmas cards before I get to her desk.)

Memory: Reporting on Books

RICHARD (on a book of Lincoln, reread by him). There was Lincoln and Washington. Washington was rich. I'm for the rich guy. No, I guess I'm for Lincoln. Here is Lincoln's house, where he was born . . . here he is whitewashing a house for his new mother. Now he goes away from home; here in New Orleans—that's the South—he's watching them sell them slaves at the block.

(Turns the page angrily, then has to turn back as the children say, "Let me see." He says in a mutter:)

Yeah, take a look. They wouldn't do that to me, boy. I wouldn't be no slave.

OTHERS. That's right.

RICHARD. Never try it with me, boy.

TEACHER. No, that was long ago; there were slaves, but Lincoln and the northern armies set them free. And many slaves fought for their own freedom.

(Children: "Make him show that picture.")

144

TEACHER. Please show the children, Richard. The picture shows how Lincoln felt. See the tears in his eyes.

CHILDREN. No, he never forgot seein that. Yes, he is crying.

RICHARD. I don't see no tears. Nobody'd do that to me.

REGGIE. I'd never sit on the back of no bus, neither.
—My great-grandfather was a slave, one of them was! The other was an Indian, so I'm kin to Indians, and no redskin can ever call me paleface.
—You don't know he was Indian.
—I *know he was*. He fought in the war.

REGGIE. Like cowboys and Indians.
—Yeah, only he was in the Cibil War, it was *real*. We got his sword.
—I wouldn't be a slave for no one, man.

TEACHER. No one is a slave today. There were slaves; they fought and became free. There are *now no slaves*.
But a long, distracted argument can't be stopped.

MONTY

One afternoon when Monty had been absent three weeks, I went to his house. He answered the door, ducking his head down when he made out my face in the corridor gloom. You can't see the corners in halls of these old-law tenement buildings, lit by 25-watt bulbs if any. I've heard from teachers in new schools that children don't want seats in the sunlight, at first.

Most mothers would not let the ten-year-old answer the door in these buildings, but Monty's dares not leave him alone with the babies even for a minute. He hurried ahead of me in his off-gait, embarrassed way, to where his mother waited on the sofa in the living room at the end of the hall. Shades were pulled down; a sliver of sun was trying to get in under one edge of a shade behind the TV set. A baby looked silently out from a crib in another corner. A second baby was asleep in her lap. She went on combing its hair but looked up sideways at me, as Monty does, waiting for me to speak first.

Yes, the Welfare came yesterday; she got the shoes, she said in an indistinct voice. "He sure did want to come back. I couldn' get the money before." She feels ashamed and guilty, yet it's nothing she has done.

145

Monty had gone out of the room and now returned, looking toward the TV set, but holding up the new shoes so I would know he'd be back tomorrow. They were large, clumsy yellow clodhoppers that no kid in the class would wear. Then he handed up from beside the sofa the old pair, with seams split all the way around each sole. One sole was gone. In other words, he had been walking through slush in one stocking foot. His mother watched, not really understanding what he was showing me or why I was looking. I was telling him to oil them down with vaseline or any kind of grease at night, until he could get galoshes. She watched how Monty listened, nodded, and left the room at once carrying the shoes, to find oil. The door closed behind him, and I saw the hanger of clean, ironed boy's shirts that hung on it. Often there aren't closets in these flats. She has always done the best she could for him.

When Monty walked into class next morning with a new haircut he was greeted with, "Heyy, y'gots a wide seam there, boy," and "Hey, what ya got—strangers in your head?" He was wearing a shirt and tie, but two or three T shirts underneath to keep him warm. On his feet the big yellow shoes, shiny with lubricating oil. "Hey, where'd *those* come from, Monty baby? John's Bargain Store?" He didn't answer. But at noon, passing my desk, muttered something out of the corner of his mouth about how busy he'd been at their house last night, scrubbing floors. He said, "I thought I'd never get back."

He comes in a few minutes early from lunch and jerks into his seat, where he sits pushing fists in his eyes to keep back tears. Richard knows why. Mrs. Cavalling said to him in lunchroom, "Well, you done playing hooky, I see. Finish with that story about the shoes?" She knows how many babies, who is working and who's not, in every family in school. In the yard, Monty had to fight about the shoes again. Took on boys, one by one. He thought he'd come back to the room and be alone; he has to let it out and cry at his desk, coat over his head. But not in front of *them.* He had defended himself.

Other Mothers. Administration

Mrs. Hervine and I give a semester reading test in our rooms; "Just for fun, just to practice," I tell the children, "but do the best you can." Josie pushed her pencil five minutes and put her head down. She scored zero. I wrote her

146

mother that if she doesn't get remedial work, she may not pass in June.

She comes in fast. "You know she was held back last year, lady. She's passin, all right. But I wanta know why she's not learnin to read. Look here, you babes went to college. You oughta be able to teach."

TEACHER. She'll have to put in more time, at home or with Miss Myles.

MOTHER. Well, I don't get it. She's been in this school four years. How come she can't read?

TEACHER. She's developed no learning habits, Mrs. Livingston. She still leaves the room four times in a morning. I'd like to send home a little list of sight words for her to work on every evening, not to the point where it will tire her but—

MOTHER. She's not stayin after and not gonna be tied up at home at night. I thought you were better than some of them. You had her out with you three times. But she's gotta learn to read in school. If she don't learn this term, it's your doin, not mine.

This interview took place in the teachers' lounge, where Bowser sat smoking a cigarette and watching out of the corner of her eye. I sank down in the other chair. "You really think that lady came to see *you,* dear? I know you sent the note, and all that. But didn't you dig the bouffant and the blue chiffon? She was on her way down the street to get herself a little something. Just dropped in here on the way."

Time: 3:05.
Scene: on the way to the office with a Form 407 (a truant slip) on Donald, who has been gone all afternoon.

(Racket of high heels. A white woman is coming up the hall, dragging Donald behind her slacks.)

TEACHER. Donald! Four children have been out looking for you this afternoon. This 407 is on its way to the office for *you.*

MOTHER. No, *I'm* lookin for *you,* lady.

(We are now outside several offices. Aides peer alertly. Inside a door, Mrs. Peliss, writing. Miss Lamb had thought she quit.)

147

TEACHER. Donald has played hooky three times this week.

MOTHER. What d'you mean, hooky? I'm the mother. Don't you think *I'd* know where he is?

MRS. WILSON (first-grade teacher, coming to door). Excuse *me*. Donald has been helping me this afternoon, Miss Burke; so don't say he's been playing hooky. He said you gave him permission, and Donald never lies.

TEACHER. I would never give a child permission to be gone all day. He was truant three times this week, and I'm making out a report on him.

MOTHER. You see, the same old thing. I'm sick and tired of it. You're all starting this stuff on him again. I'm taking him out of this goddamned school.

TEACHER. Four children were sent down to get him, and he still didn't return.

WILSON. He *was not playing hooky.* You did *not send* down four children for him.

MRS. HALLOWELL (white-haired assistant to district superintendent, putting her hat on, comes out of the office.) Please, ladies, what is going on here? *Please* step into the principal's office with me.

(All enter office, meeting principal.)

DONALD (pleased). Hello, Mr. Saltz, this is my little cousin.

SALTZ. Hello, little cousin. (Walks out.)

TEACHER. Mrs. Hallowell, this boy has been absent ten half-days.

MOTHER. I'm the mother. Don't listen to her! Don't you think the mother would know if her oldest is absent? I know when I send him out where he goes, so I don't know what *you're* sayin. I'm the mother.

WILSON (nods). That's true.

MOTHER. So don't you think the mother would know? The mother sends the child out in the morning; the mother *knows*.

(Miss Rippley, head aide, steps out of another office, all in violet with matching headband. Long pause as she mentally records the exact skin color of baby in Mrs. Downey's arms.)

148

RIPPLEY. Donald is all over this school. I hate to say it, dear, but he is. I know you would want to know this. I consistently see the child in the hall.

(Donald, behind mother, raises his hand.)

Yes, Mrs. Downey, Donald has been seen on second floor, on third floor; I see him on various floors and say to myself, "Doesn't that child have a class to go to?" though I know in my heart he has.

(Miss Lionni approaches. Pauses reluctantly.)

TEACHER. Miss Lionni, four monitors were sent down this afternoon to find this boy.

WILSON. Four monitors were *not*.

MOTHER. You see, every one of them lying; no wonder he can't get anywhere. Do you think a mother should have to stand and listen to lies about her child? I'm the mother.

TEACHER. Miss Lionni, the boy is in my room; he's on my register. What is the procedure on this? Is he to be out without my permission?

LIONNI (who is taking assistant-principal exam in May). I—I really must—

(Steps away in direction taken by Mr. Saltz, who is now chasing children out of front hall.)

HALLOWELL. There is *one* procedure. If he is registered in your room, he may not be gone without your permission.

MOTHER. You see? Every damn one of them, picking on my kids ever since they been in this school. I'm takin them both out.

(Snatches Donald. Wilson and mother walk off together, talking wildly.)

Teaching. No Effort. No Attention

Harold is the first finished and has three wrong. Teacher: "When you've corrected these, you may read a library book." Harold: "I finished it, so why do I have to correct it?"

He corrects, with tears in his eyes, jabbing the pencil. Breaks the pencil. Then an argument over what to read: "Get a book from the library table." "I read all of 'em."

"You read them or you looked at the pictures? . . . Please go get one. . . . Try the story of the lost sailor." "I read it."

Josie's head is down. I've seen her fall asleep in the sun on a bench outside. Utter exhaustion.

Reggie finishes and wants to talk about his new boots.

Teacher: "No, the third problem's wrong—do you see? You added; you didn't multiply. Reggie, please look at the paper. The third problem. Look at what the paper says: three eights are twenty-four; four sixes are twenty-four; two twelves are—?" Repeat. He clamps his lips shut, digs his boot heel in the floor. The button in his head has turned off. He wants to be left alone. Can't watch the numbers. "Please watch my tens frame." Suddenly he clenches his teeth, grabs the paper, stomps back to his desk.

Mrs. Weiss and I stand at the classroom door. "I don't know where to start or finish. That's what I didn't expect. Two weeks ago, five children could do long and short vowels. Now, none of the five know all the vowels. And math. That's the best thing they do. Now I find out they can't do it—today, I say, 'Three twos are six, *five* twos (they expect "four") are—?' Silence."

Mrs. Weiss: "I've gone through it year after year. You think you're batting a thousand—then it blows up on you. They've forgotten everything. No one of them is ever with the school scene."

"Mrs. Weiss, what are they doing? Look at them. What is Reggie doing right now? What is Malcolm doing? Look how they're sitting. Doing nothing because I've stepped out of the door—is that it?"

Not even any noise in the room. Most children have stopped work and sit with vacant stares. Malcolm is looking out the window, his mouth open slack. He is looking on a blank courtyard. There is nothing out there. Reggie is hunched in his seat, angry tears in his eyes. He wanted to talk about the after-shave lotion he was wearing; I had told him to open his reader. He is ruined for the day.

"I thought Virgil was really ticking. He can read. Last week he knew homonyms. When there's a correlation he sees it, shouts it out. Today, I asked him to correct a Rexographed sheet. 'No, I'm not gonna.' *'Virgil. What is it?'* Something is always eating them. No one can correct anything. They take it as a personal insult—they've given me the sheet; what do I want from them now? Won't try, can't bear to fail."

Mrs. Weiss: "It's always the children with problems who can't read. For most of these children, life is a burden that

150

they want to put down. They are really very sad children. And the school doesn't work for them. The curriculum has to be overhauled. They hate school; they really do.

"And what comes next for your babies? Sick Jefferson. Jefferson is the terminal date. Kids give each other fixes and have sex in the washrooms, at Jefferson. You know that in the spring there aren't so many wars and rumbles around here any more; the thing is cool it, go on the needle. I know your kids say, 'I ain't goin to Jefferson, that's a *bad* school'; but actually they will—for a while. Then most of them will drop out."

The Truant Officer

One afternoon, weeks after the truant reports had gone out on Curtis and Ernie, I was in the back of the room where a fight was raging. Someone had snatched someone else's sandwich at noon. "Your teeth so rotten they're crumbly and flaky, and so's your mother's. Your mother's teeth, they're almost not there." "Double for *your* mother's teeth. Your mother's an addic'." "Well, yours's a whore, and she wears iron drawers with barb wire trimmins." More. Then a sudden silence fell on the room. The fight stopped. Leanore, who has been taking mornings off again lately, dropped quietly in her seat.

The truant officer had entered, and when I'd returned to my desk we talked for a few minutes. He kept the children under his eye, and they stared back at his stickpin in a dark tie with whorls running in it, the cut of his suit, his cuff links. They do not often see a Negro man like this. I said, "I'm sorry I had to send out so many notices. But too much work has been put into these boys. Miss Myles, Mrs. Weiss, myself. Not to pick them up now would be like dropping them in a sewer."

"Oh no, I'm glad you did. As you see, I can't keep up with my truant notices. We always have a backlog of months. I've been to see Curtis and Ernie since last night. Neither place answered the bell."

Vernon: "Hey, I'll take you where Ernie *really* lives! He's back at his mother's! But we gotta go there *real* late, she ain't there till late. Ernie neither."

The officer continued, "Donald's mother was to escort him to school today—oh, she didn't? Well, we can have her in court. Once he's back we'll put a special officer on him to see there's no deviation. Curtis?"

"Curtis just goes home, into a pocket. For him, it's bet-

151

ter than being in school. His mother doesn't care."

"Today I've had three mothers lie to me for their kids: measles, hospital, measles. No father, any of the three. I wish there were more of us. But we're just machinery. The State can't replace parents."

He then asked the class if anyone had seen the three boys.

REGGIE. I'm walkin along; it was Saturday night, I gots my new boots on! Who do I see—Ernie! Ernie looked *good*. I say, "Ernie, man, where y'been?" We talkkk! I'm with my girl, so after a while we break up, but then I see Curtis! Curtis didn't look so good, had on ol' bleach pants and a broke-down Army cap; he looked bad. Looked like he was sniffin glue. He says he *never comin back*. Ernie you couldn't tell so much. He say he was afraid to come back now.

"They always are, after they're out a few weeks," said the officer to me, and to Reggie, "See if you can't get him back to school, son."

The officer then talked to William and Leanore, bending down beside each of them. They squirmed but listened. "Have you been in court before? This jig-jag course leads you to the court. I'm not here to intimidate you or make you fearful. But the law says you must be in school. That's what you must understand. Your place is not at home doing laundry or watching babies, but here. Tell your mothers you can only do home chores after three o'clock. Each day in this room follows up what you did yesterday. You must be here, doing your best."

VERNON. Listen, I seen Ernie too and I talked a lot longer to him than Reggie. I said, "When we move to the new school we're leavin you behind." Ernie didn't know the new plan, see, that we're kickin all truants out. He got *mad*. He was on his way fishin but he say, "You can't keep me outa no school. I'm gonna be right in that new school with you."

When the officer had gone, a talk on law and justice branched out.

LEANORE. Stay outa those courts, boy. My mother goes often. It's okay, but it gets on your nerves. You gotta wear really good shoes, the kind your mother buys when she says, "I want you to get some *good* shoes, the kind that'll take a lot of punishment"; and a beautiful stick-up dress, so the judge don't look down over the bench and say, "Well, look how she's dressed! What do you want from the child?"

152

—My aunt and uncle warrin and feudin. The judge sent 'em away, say he don't want no feudin.

JOSIE.   *I* gots to go to courts tomorrow.

CLAUDE.   Teacher, mah pencil's goh'n.

VERNON.   Listen, *we're goin to court* a week from today. I was hit by a car; my mother is suing that woman for five hundred dollars. And if she don't get that money to pay my mother, my mother gettin that car and is it beyewtifulll! All pink and red inside. My father knows how to drive and he's learnin my mother how to drive.

JASON.   My brother got one thousand dollars; his knee-cap got busted by a bus, and we're gettin a tape recorder, a transistor, and a typewriter. But my mother ain't leavin the money at home. She's taking it to work and leave it on her desk.

LEANORE.   Never lie or steal. You can't tell *just one lie.* First you've got to back up lie number one with number two; then before you know it you've told number three to back *that* up, and you're telling number four and five to back up number one.
(To me) a thief will take *rubies*—suppose that kind of rubies Mrs. Weiss wears—he'll take one, put it in a hock shop. And the man puts the glass in his eye and says, "Where'd you get it?" And the guy says, "Wellll, we've had a lot of *deep* trouble at home, my wife's very sick and she's expecting, and my sister's got a bad bladder," and many other things he'll say. By the time he's through, the man takes that glass out of his eye. He *knows.* But he don't care, you see. He might need that ring too.

VERNON.   You gotta have your own money for your own sugar, if you goes to jail.

CLAUDE.   Teacher, Ah've nev-ah been in no jail.

A week ago Claude's records came up and it turned out he was from Alabama, not Mississippi at all. "It's Floradell, *Alabama,* then, Claude?" A happy smile crossed his face. Something in the name sounded familiar. "And we don't have the date of your birthday, Claude. When is that?" He thinks very hard, screwing up one eye so every dimple comes into play. "About what time of year? Spring? Perhaps around Christmas time? . . ."
This idea he liked, but we could get no closer to the real

153

day. After other questions, he says, "Mah birthday's down south."

On a later day he reveals, "Ma'm, Ah didn't *go* to school for a rah't long time. Ah had to watch those children for that widow lady, cause they burnt that ol' shack down. When she hang up wash, I gots to be there at that *new* shack." (Children nod: "That's right.")

VERNON (to Josie). How come you talks in a whisper to Claude?

JOSIE. That's how you gots to talk to him.

(As Claude is speaking, she puts her ear almost to his lips. He tells of the three mules.)

CLAUDE. One was Rowww-dy . . . one called Pah'son . . . one name Mawww'd. Mawwwd was a reddd mewlll . . . th*row*'ed me off her back. Mah fathah say, "That reddd mewlll ain' goan let *no*-body rides her."

TEACHER. The red mule must have been very exciting.

CLAUDE (pause). No, ma'am. She was the-ah every day.

(In a later discussion of the South:)

CLAUDE. No, they be some *nice* white people in the South. You be walkin down that road—

MONTY (to himself). That ol' dusty road—

CLAUDE. And white folk rah'd by, and waves rah't to the colored folk, and we waves rah't back.

(Children imitate throwing up.)

REGGIE. I wouldn't walk on no road. Or ride the back of no bus, neither.

MONTY. How would whites people like it if colors rode all in the front, made 'em stand up? They'd be so sad, they couldn't think of nothing except how they was bein pushed on the back of that bus.

REGGIE. Hey stupid, it was the other way around. The coloreds got to sit in the back, but no more. Martin Luthern King made 'em walk; now they *don't* sit there.

(This sets off a fight. William is throwing his fists in the air, neither understands the argument nor can stand it. "I'm not sittin there, not me!")

RICHARD. Look, William, no one's makin' you sit there, they had to quit.

(Later.)

RUBY. Before Martin Luther King there wasn't nobody to help those people in the South go to the zoo and ride the ferris wheel.

—Martin Luther King is fighting for civil war.

—No, *civil rights*. The reason the colored people is getting so nervous now and Martin Luther King works for them is, they wants their own President.

—He didn't do nothin when they wanted to fight him in that motel. He's not that kinda stupid guy. He like to start everything with a prayer. He is a Christian boy all the way, and he is a doctor that leads the people. And that's the kinda doctor he is.

Donald is still out and the children are cleaning out desks for Christmas. Jason and Harold take out the contents of Donald's desk:

Magazines.

A catalogue for metal machinery parts. Pages stuck together with chocolate and other food.

Three-color picture in newspaper supplement of semi-nude girl as Santa's helper. It is folded in a hundred creases, stuck together with yellow globs.

A 1924 geography book: pictures of children in knickers and buckled coats visiting children of Holland, Switzerland, etc. Rotogravure of Eskimos in front of an igloo, beige background. Given by some teacher, also cleaning out room at end of year.

Old neuter-color songbook containing such songs as "Little Sir Echo" and cover-stamp illustration of woman in bare feet, flowing hair, carrying banner "America, America." Leanore paged through this and said, "Gee, I don't know any of these songs."

Candy wrappers.

Sears Roebuck catalogue with heads in pictures cut out.

Sixth-grade phonics workbook, diacritical marks over words.

A 1962 calendar and appointment and memoranda book for the day scribbled with gibberish on each page.—A pamphlet on the "White-Fringe Beetle and How To Control It," and one on the "Soybean Cyst Nematode."

A cap that had been found on top of our cabinet.

An *Esquire* with an interview of Belle Starr in a gold G-string.

Pomade is on every newspaper and magazine in Donald's desk; it is smeared on the blackboard behind him.

VERNON. Donald's been helpin' his father; his father owns the supermarket.

MONTY. Yeah, since when'd he get a father? Sometimes it's his uncle. He oughta make up his mind.

—Listen, Donald knows all those po-lice. Last night he was goin right down the block in the squad; he was settin right up in front next to Captain Riley. He report you to that captain if he want to. Gave a big ol' wave out that window.

RICHARD. Yeah, he better watch out he don't report no Jefferson boys. If they get sent to the Home, they lay for you the rest of your life. It's a funny thing. Those cops all helps Donald whatever he wants. If a big boy took his money, he just go to the cop on my corner, but if I goes to him at the end he always say, "I'm sorry but you better run along now, son. Run home."

Dancing

If all work is finished by two on Friday, the children may dance until three. Everybody conscientiously brings records—some, three or four. One child brings his mother's favorite, Mahalia Jackson singing "Silent Night," and a few children titter. None of the records are the best: older brothers and sisters need them. Up in front, the children look over the records and pretty much agree. Nothing dated. Reggie sneaked out with the best one today, Martha and the Vandellas' "There He Is." He takes over the record player. No arguments.

Each child listens a few seconds, getting the beat. Then grabs the partner he likes. The boys dance with each other, as do the girls. Later they start mixing. Two or three children no one chooses, and these don't choose each other. Vernon leads off; he picked up a good step from his seventh-grade sister last night. Two rows of boys stand and follow him dancing up front. All smiling but concentrating, fingers snapping, catching every other beat. No one misses a beat.

Reggie does some bright steps; the others fall back. Instantly he's leading. Harold (who doesn't dance) calls, "Reggie, do the Grime!"

—Grime ain't for kids, that's a nasty dance! Teen-agers do the Grime and the Dog; they get really close to the boy!

156

Try different nasty things, but they sure can do a lot of dances! Dance in front of the drugstore in my block; the light's on late.

—Children not supposed to do the Grime or the Dog. Dance with your own group.

LEANORE. My sister and me watch my mother and her friends; she *really* knows how to do the Grime, but boy, she don't want me doin' it.

—My mother does it at parties; making a party this Saturday night. Going to wear her red silk shoes. Makin macaroni, and maybe my father coming. I can't wait.

—Let's do the Mouse. I seen a guy on TV doin it. He could really do it! Watch me!

—No, we're gonna do the Jerk!

Reggie, Claude, and Virgil step out in the Jerk. The whole body moves but not the feet. Never touch your partner. Shut your eyes or cast them up.

—Hey, that's good! That's really good! Play that again!

—Keep that on!

Josie dances out of her seat as the Supremes go on ("You Beat Me to the Punch")—throws me a wink.

CASSIE. You be mirthful, teacher!

Then *she* can't stand it any longer and dances into the Jerk. She's so good, Malcolm dances up to her, follows her.

—Put on the Vandellas again!

—Hey Malcolm, watcha doin there, the Wobble?

MALCOM (dancing). This ain't the Wobble, but my mother still does the Wobble. Don't care if you say, "No one wobbles any more," she say, "I like to wobble." I say "Don't do it any more; it's out of style," and my father laugh his head off! She goes on doin it!

RICHARD. Stop doin the Dog, William!

—I bet your sister do that, William!

RICHARD (dancing). Hey, stop the Dog.

—Ernie did that in third grade when the teacher was gone. Slipped back to his seat fast, but she could tell something happened by our faces!

VERNON (*dancing*). Can't even do it anyway. Don't know what he's doin.

—There ain't *no* dance *I* can't do.

RUBY (changing records). "Baby Love!" The Supremes!

—Here's the Popeye.

—Boston Monkey. Do this on my street.

—Dig Noah! He's dancin the Frug!
—Hey, Noah, that was last year!
—Show me the Uncle Willie.
—That's nothin' special. Just where you start out.

VERNON. Just this. (Dances a side step.) Anybody can do it.
Every child participates except the four loners. Dancers
step back and watch just a few seconds—when someone's
the best, or they want to pick up the step themselves. Iris
is too big; she gets in a corner and sits there. Roger stares
from his seat. Harold watches, then decides to go up and
wash the blackboard. Donald stands muttering, "I don't
know what to do. I wanta do it, too."

MONTY. Put my record on: "The Way You Do the Things
You Do." "Temptations." Record we dance in Lonnie Long's.

—No, put on "There He Is" again!

Records change, and Richard says to Ruby, "May I have
this dance?" which cracks up everyone, but four boys instantly copy him, "May I have this dance" to other girls,
and cutting-in starts. Mostly with Cassandra. Ruby calls,
"Oh, I wish we could dance forever!"

RICHARD. Wouldn't do some of those dances if you dance
in church. My minister say he let some dancing go on in
our church; God don't mind if its clean and slow. Clap
your hands soft. But the kids don't wanta do them too much,
slow dances.

VIRGIL. Martin Luther King wouldn't dance like that.

MALCOLM. Get outa here; he don't dance at all. Too busy
goin to too many events.

RICHARD. Oh, I think he might dance if it's nice and slow.
—In summer, almost everyone in my block dances on the
street every night. We stay out really late!
—Put on the Supremes! They are the best!
—They light people, but they sing like us.

TEACHER. You mean white people?
—Light people! No such thing as white people; paper is
white, but people only light and dark. But Supremes as light
as you.

Approach of Christmas

Children are wearing Christmas presents in advance:
socks, flannel shirts, mittens. Josie has on a blue knitted

hood. "How pretty! Is that for Christmas?" Josie (angrily): "No, she just want me to be warm." Reggie has new rubber boots like the ones the construction men wear. Sometimes doesn't hear his name when you call. He is staring at the boots; sticks them up on the desk in front of him.

VERNON. He can't *never* take 'em off. My mother says it'll make his brain soft.

MALCOM. He's wearin 'em night and day. He'll get gangarene or cancer, if he don't let some air get at those feet.

REGGIE. It ain't worryin' me none.

Sign on stair wall: "I want a bushel of Pusy for Christmas." On 116th and 125th Street, some bunting strung across. But few lights in people's windows. Here and there, a very small tree, no lights (fire hazard).
Less money than usual. The children always have pennies jingling but never forty or fifty cents to go to Rockefeller Center to see lights on great trees. Only a few children do go. Monty brings a message from his mother: "She want me to go, but can I bring the money Saturday. She think she can lay her hands on some Friday night."

HAROLD. We're goin to my aunt's in Brooklyn. *She* got lights.

WILLIAM. We ain't poor! No! My father sends money for me every week! Christmas we're havin collard greens, macaroni, roast chicken, two chocolate cakes, soda pop for dessert.
—It says in the Bible, God's birthday is on Christmas.
—Jews don't believe in Christmas and that's the truth. Jewish children wake up on Christmas morning and say to their mother, Let's have a nice Christmas, like the colored folk.

MONTY. I don't see how they gets along without Christmas. I wish it was Christmas ev-ery day.

Stealing

When the plants died, the children were very upset. *"Reggie and Vernon* killed them, they was touching them every day." "That's a lie! It was that old radiator!"
Richard and William are sent to the dime store to get a new plant for Christmas.

RICHARD. William wanted to take the first flower he saw. Not me. You got to get one that won't die. We've got more than a flower here, we've got a plant. Had William keep guard, took my time. We paid. But the big boys come after us anyway, walkin on their heels behind us. We had to run! It's this Christmas time coming. All the teen-age boys in Jefferson, they want money for their girl friends' Christmas presents. They are *laying* for you!

—*They gets it with knives*, K55. They lookin to buy her a present. Carry your money in your underwear, teacher, or in you socks! Those boys dangerous, put the knife up to you; they put it to little kids and say, Your money or your life!

—Teen-agers they break in those wine stores on the weekend. They need the money, wanta go buy those three-quarters coats that look like leather.

CASSANDRA. My little brother, he goin to the sto'. And they try to tuk his money. But Ruby called, "Andy, here come your father!" They let him alone.

RICHARD. If you're smart, have some money on you. Take out and give them some; maybe they go away.

—When you steal in the dime store, he takes you in that room and beats you. But it's his business; he can do that. Either the white guy beats you or that colored guy. Dime store's almost goin out of business, they steal so much.

—In John's Bargain Store there's a guy doesn't do *nothing* but chase stealers.

—No, he help unpack boxes too sometimes. But mostly he chases stealers.

—Marty copped a can of pork and beans in the A & P. I was a witness. Put it under his arm in his jacket. Then he got real loud up in front and yell at me, "Hey, kid, what'd y'steal?" And laughed and run!

REGGIE. Go into Blumstein's you can only go wich your mother; they're afraid you'll steal.

RICHARD. Man you are *storyin!* That is *you;* you was touchin somethin!

—Stealing chips, that's easy. One of you talks to the man, gets him in back; friend takes the chips. The man stays up in front, when you come in he say, "What d'you want? Don't hang around in here, kid. You gonna buy something? Where's your money?"

REGGIE. You steals what you needs and you can't gets.

LEANORE. My father came home with his Christmas bonus in advance last night, hundred dollars on him, having a good time, got drunk, and winos got it. Got the hundred in that hall, put a knife up my mother's back. She had the money. Someone called the cops, though, and my mother pushed 'em right in the paddy wagon with a broom. They were so drunk, she handled 'em; but, then, she handles everything. She didn't even want my father around, only that hundred. When it was all over, she said, "I'd like a couple of people to clear out for tonight." He left. And I'm going down to my grandma's tonight, turn on that TV.

"Around Here"

Malcolm has the job of watching for stealers in the grocery. "I watch for the guy lookin nice and easy. Tell my boss."

VIRGIL. I show people around the furniture store, but I got fired yesterday cause I didn't show up on time. Cause I had to stay after school. But I went out and met my friends givin out leaflets in the subway. They asked the boss man if I could help. Made a dollar.

MONTY. I work in a bakery and get the broken cookies.
REGGIE. Sweep out a guy's basement and pull down the garbage for the super.

MALCOLM. In summer, I help my father pick up old iron, and he helps people move. And sell some fish—porgies, whiteys, eels, butterfish. Some watermelons. But we drops that in the winter.

Curtis and Ernie buy the *News* for seven cents, sell it for ten, mostly 125th Street, where the men in bars are their friends.

LEANORE. Ernie's gettin' mad at Curtis, though. Curtis does all the planning, then makes Ernie pull the dirty work.

CURTIS: He say that?

LEANORE. He did.

CURTIS. I don't know why. I never sound on his sniffin glue.

(Harold is crying, because he doesn't have Christmas money.)

TEACHER. Why don't you get a newspaper route like the two boys?

HAROLD. I only got a quarter. How many newspapers could you buy with that?

TEACHER. Why don't you ask Curtis?

HAROLD. Curtis ain't gonna tell you nothin.

MALCOLM. And Ernie said he's quittin anyway. He was saving for that deep-sea pole, but three times in a month the big boys took everything. He say, "Why should I go out in the cold, lose it all. Even if I get to my house, they get me."

JASON. My mother made me stop sellin.

MALCOLM. And Curtis betrayed Ernie again.

ERNIE (speaks up). Well, I almost had the ten dollars for that pole.

RICHARD (laughs). Yeah, Ernie always has to get the *best*.

LEANORE. Yes, you could get one for two dollars, then get yourself a new shirt.

ERNIE. Well, you did betray me, Curtis. Your cousin come and you betrayed me.

CURTIS. The reason is you can't keep up fast enough, and we got to go a lot of places.

ERNIE. You're a liar. I ain' good enough for you when your cousin comes. Y'do it all the time.

CURTIS. You are. Y'live in a dump. Nothin but old broke bottles and winos in your hall. Any big fight, the cops go right to your building. Your mother's a wino. You stay outa Melody Bar. Those are my customers.

(Later.)

TEACHER (to Ernie). But can't you put your money in your shoe?

(Children laugh.)

MALCOLM. You can't put it nowhere. They take off your shoes, your socks; they get in your underwear; they want everything. Don't dare come from the store with groceries like you got any money left. They go every place on you. (To

162

the others) You know Jack? Mean guy, all raggy; when he come on that playground everyone get down off things and run away?

("Real blackeye? Stands at 121st Street? I know him.")

MALCOLM. Well, he's one the guys got Ernie Saturday night. He hit the street; they seen him takin papers out; they wait till he sold. It was raining; he didn't get rid of his pack till after midnight. Money from twenty papers.

TEACHER. But you can't let them take it! You have to fight back, defend yourselves!

VERNON. You kiddin? They sniffin glue. You can't mess with a sniffer! Glue tear your lungs out. A sniffer's *wild*.

VIRGIL. Best thing is try to jump into the middle of the street; but if I can't dodge 'em, shake my head in and out, go this way, that way, hide behind cars, run in and out! Act like I'm nuts, just crazy. You gotta do your best. I push this way, that way, I punches, I bangs out. I'm gonna get it one day.

Stealing spreads into the room. Children want me to frisk others.

TEACHER. I'm not frisking anyone. I'm not a policeman. I ought to be able to leave a dime on this desk if I want to; it's my desk. Monty, would you look in the coats; perhaps the dime's in one of them.

RICHARD. Yeah, but you better make sure you're not tuckin it in there to get rid of it, Monty. You're supposed to be takin it out.

—It's not enough, Miss Burke. You got to frisk every kid. You got to have everyone put their hands on their head. Go in everywhere, underwears and everywhere. If you don't stop this now, it won't never stop and it'll be your own fault.

—Listen to their heart. If it goes *ptump-ptump-ptump*, they're lying. If it goes *pump, pump, pump,* that's different.

—The guy whose eyeballs are doin things, or else aren't doin much, is the one you want.

—It's gotta stop, and you got to stop it, Miss Burke. You got to get to the bottom of it. Look in the loop of the boys' pants; they balances money there. Go into their socks.

CASSIE. Wouldn't be surprised if Reggie tuk it; he look so spry helpin Mr. Wilcox take that liz'hd out. And he's smokin. If a puh'son smokes, that pur'son'll do anything.

(Later. Noon. Again, Ernie went out with papers last
night and was robbed.)

TEACHER. Please, let's find out if you can't open an account and put your money in it right away.

ERNIE. No. I'm quittin.

VERNON. They *gets* it right away, don't you understand?
They watch when you *get* your papers, lay for you. Too
lazy to sell their own.
 --Teacher, you don't mean wrong, I know, but you don't
know what it's like around here. It's just not the same as
where you live. This is nothin against New York; a lot of
parts are nice, but we got the bad part, around here.

TEACHER. How about selling across the park?

VERNON. Oh yeah, Morningside. White people's section, I
know where it is.

TEACHER (to Curtis). You and Ernie could open little ac-
counts over there. I'll go with you.

CURTIS. On your side of town?

TEACHER. Yes, or how about the Freedom Bank on 125t'
Street?

CURTIS. No. Where you live.

ERNIE (thinking about it). It means cross that park . . .
you'd have to get a flashlight to come back. Well, I'll see tonight. I'm gettin my billy back tonight; I don't care. If they
steal after tonight, I'm quittin.

(Ernie turns and goes to the back of the room, where
boys are talking.)

CURTIS (remains). I'm gettin me a knife.

RICHARD. Yeah? What if the cops catch you with it?

(Laughs and gets up and leaves. He, too, goes to the
back.)

CURTIS. Well, I ain't gonna use it . . . (Softly, after-
thought) unless I has to. . . . But I'm thinkin of quittin
When I gets home, she say, "Currie, share your money
with James." I tell her, "Let him get his own." She say
"Currie, don't be so mean. Give James a little that money
or I'll give him a lot of it, Currie." Does that all the
time. But I don't care. I had a knife before, and when I

164

was goin to bed, my brother said, "Gimme some of that money." I pushed him into the dresser. I got into bed. Then I kept lookin at my knife. I was gonna—I was gonna do this—(He shows how he put the knife to his chest.)

TEACHER. You mean, to your brother?

CURTIS (softly). No, I meant *for me*.

TEACHER. Curtis, what do you mean? What would happen to the rest of us? Who draws all the beautiful pictures— the bands of Greek soldiers, the birds, the butterflies for the class?

CURTIS. I dunno.

TEACHER. Look around the room—think of the happiness you've given all of us.

CURTIS. Someone else can do it. I don't care.

(In the back of the room, Monty and Ernie are in a fight.)

ERNIE. I'm comin' to see my cousin. He got my billy.

MONTY. Stay off my street. I'll kill you.

ERNIE. Yeah? What'd I ever do to you?

MONTY. Just don't come on my street, I don't care who you're comin to see, you won't get beyond that corner.

HAROLD (in front). The fights in here, like cats and dogs. A dog'll take a bite. A cat'll take a bite.

JASON. Some kids say, I wish I was never born.

LEANORE (who has been listening through the long conversation of the boys). It's funny, I don't understand. If God knows everything and he knowed it would be like this, why he let you be borned anyway? When God birthed you, you were sweet and dear. But before he can turn around, he sees a bum has growed up. Even he doesn't know how it happened. But I guess it happens just around here.

Teachers at the End of the Year

All the children in my class have quit Miss Myles. Other clubs dwindle. Some teachers are weary.

Four teachers are quitting after Christmas. Striack's father

165

said he'd buy her a little car in the spring; she can teach in the suburbs. Another new teacher is leaving to go to Harvard Graduate School. More subs in the halls; some quit at noon and don't come back.

Big complaints over projected New Math in-training for teachers after January. Teachers would attend during lunch hour. Some are checking to see if it's legal, if the union can't stop it. Others are getting up a petition. "I'm simply not going. What do they expect of us?"

Bowser met Donald Downey in the hall yesterday taking back to his dear friend, Mrs. Wilson, her bowl with a china robin, sans philodendron lent to him after the upsetting scene with his mother that day.

"But where's the plant, dear?" said Bowser. "I bet you forgot to bring it from home. Just bring it tomorrow in a little bag, dear, but take the bowl on in to Mrs. Wilson now—I know she'll be glad to have it back."

WILSON.   That was a twenty-five-dollar vase. You'd think his mother could have at least washed the inside out. That bird's wing was broken.

BOWSER.   Maybe his mother used it as a salad bowl, honey, or made a nice philodendron salad.

WILSON.   What?

BOWSER.   I said, who knows what it was used for, dear.

WILSON.   Oh, come on.

The 'Tarded Teacher is quitting and told Mr. Goff, "Better for all concerned."

Christmas Preparations

Josie: "We'se givin you a surprise party for Christmas. I'se collected two dollars and forty-six cents." She tells me this twice a day or more. On a Friday I tell the whole class the party's off, because while learning "The Night Before Christmas" for Assembly, Reggie, Jason, and Harold dropped their pants as they stood in the back row reciting, "Now Dancer, now Prancer, now Donner and Blitizen!" But in spite of this little contretemps Josie and others go on collecting and counting pennies. "*You* don't has to pay anything," says Josie. "I hope the boys don'ts be greedy, though and eat up the cake in five minutes like last year, then start yankin up dresses when it gets too good."

The preholiday tension rises. Many teachers out. A sub

166

stitute in second grade wanders into the teachers' lounge on the wrong floor, abstracted, red blotches on her neck. Stares at herself in the mirror, nervous tears in her eyes. Rowby's room dominates the floor. *Slam,* a girl will flip out the door dodging a boy; they race to the stairs, she falls halfway down the landing, screaming. All hours fights are going on inside or someone's talking to Rowby at the door (you get just a glimpse of his glassy-eyed lozenge-shaped face): "Well, we want to know who *is* in your class today; someone up here is ringing the fire alarm. Don't you know who's here today?" The halls are swarming. Leanore: "I never seen so many dislocated children walking around the halls as today."

Jefferson children wander in and out of the building. It is rather sad. School is the only world they have ever known outside their homes. They fear the unknown. They are looking for something to come back to. Two girls in open tennis shoes, neither with a hat, coats unbuttoned, stand in the front entrance, hugging themselves, shivering. Bitter cold weather. One girl's teeth are broken. "Shi', girl, this col' jus' stabbin me." Friend: "You don' think *I* likes it, does you?" They shiver, half-looking at each other, and talk in mumbles:

—Listen, girl, you can' come back here tomorrow. She don' wan' you in that class.

—She can' kick me out; that's my room.

—Well, she said, Annabelle. When she see that gone, she say it was you, and she's had enough; she kicking you out.

ANNABELLE. Yeah, well, I'se comin' back. She can' say it was jus' me. They four of us outa that room.

FRIEND. Well, she look around and around, and look in that drawer, Annabelle. She throw you out if you come back.

ANNABELLE. She can' kick me. I got no place to go.
FRIEND (losing interest). Don' come back; she throw you out if you do, Annabelle.

In the room, we hang up some large ornaments, mobiles of deep beautiful mauve, purple, crimson, chartreuse. They act for peace and sanity. If I say, "I'm not sure we're going to make our own ornaments," the class gets quiet. The jewels sway above the front rows. Reggie lolls back, stretching out the new boots, and looks up at the jewels floating into a magic vault.

TEACHER. An artist who's a friend of Mrs. Hervine made them, and we'll make some too, and we can make jewels like

167

them just before Christmas. Merchants hang ornaments like these in great windows downtown, to make people happy Christmas shopping. Curtis, he's an artist; he might make real ornaments like these when he grows up. He might get that kind of job . . . if he finishes school and then goes to art school. Photographers for magazines need jewels like these, too.

VERNON. But how would he get a job? How would he know?
—Where is the job?
—Who said that you go there?

REGGIE. Listen, is it true that for every job they have to wire your head to see if you can do it?
—Oh, I be so scared if they do that, I don't want a job.
—Where would you have to go to get a job?

VIRGIL. First you have to get your schooling, not be a drop-out. You have to go to school every day like Martin Luthern King did.

RICHARD. When he was little he said to his mother, "I think I have a little chest cold," and she said, "Oh, you better stay home today." But he said, "No, mother, I can't miss that school, not even a day." Wouldn't refuse a whuppin. Always thought about the colored people and that they gets their ways.

VIRGIL. Which is why he got the Nobel Peace Prize.

VERNON. Gave away every penny of it. I'd give only half. Three thousand dollars.

(Others: "No: fifty-four thousand!")

With that you could buy a boat, a Cadillac, even a house He didn't do that. Not even a wrist watch.

REGGIE. He is very honest like George Washington; when he was a kid, wouldn't skip his whupping. Washington's old father come in and say, "Who shots this tree down?" And George say, "Excuse me, sir, I don't like to say." And his father say, "I know you didn't do it." (Enacting, stands up shows George coming closer, head down.) George come in a little closer; he knows his father gonna whup him, but he say, "Excuse me, sir, I done it. I cannot tell no lie; I am like Martin Luther King."

RICHARD. He is very important and many people love him All the important heads of government want to talk to him And I'd like to be him.

168

WILLIAM. Mmm-mmm! Look at that tuxedo.

REGGIE. It is *Dino!*

TEACHER. That is a cutaway coat.

CURTIS

He began making Christmas jewels of velvet, grosgrain ribbon, silver paper. Next day at night at home, he made things of his own on construction paper—a huge Jiminy Cricket from *Pinocchio,* with crossed, dapper legs; a bird with head chalked out in white, breast of powder blue, wings flowing in many colors into midnight blue. Then he came back from lunch half an hour late, covering his ears when I tried to talk to him in the hall. *"No,* don't try that again, tellin me about the *class* all the time, *'They* came back from lunch on time, *you* didn't,' don't tell *me* what they did, I'm me, they're them. I don't hardly listen when you talk about them." In the room he wouldn't answer when called on to read, and at two o'clock I noticed that he had left his artwork on an empty seat across from him and slipped away.

MISS LIONNI (enunciating in whispers of a closed case). We're just going to let Truancy take over from now on. (Reassuring smile.) Yes, it's just their affair now, it's *for the best.* Some children simply cannot function within the structure of school. It's best to just let things take their course. My goodness, you did *all you could.*

TEACHER. No, I didn't, but he ate me alive.

LIONNI. Oh now really, you did marvelously. They have such difficult involved problems, we just *can't do any more* than our best, can we? We must live with *facts.*

The day before Christmas the school goes wild. My room is being dismissed when a bunch of sixth-grade girls, coats over their heads, rush in, pouncing on the smallest children in front, singing, "Who wantsa dance on Saturday night?" They snatch things from the children, drive Leanore shrieking out into the hall. "Where's that white boy you got in here?" and "Look at that blaaack Reggie!" "Listen woman, I wants my kid sister. What're you gonna do about it? Hit me, I dare you!" ("Don't you touch her, lady! If she touches you, Veronica—!") The littlest comes at me with sleeves of coat pulled around her head, hands out like claws: "EEEaaagh!"

Most of my children run off. Miss Myles, arriving with Leanore, goes after the girls, but they get away. Leanore wouldn't say who they were: "It wouldn't do any good Miss Burke, fussin with those girls. They'll go to Jefferson and get some more girls; then they'll all come *later* and get you. And they'll do like my mother; they'll come right *into* the situation, right into your class again. Take my advice, forget about it. (Growing angry) Don't ask me what I'm doin for Christmas. My mother's gone away, and I have to take care of her baby."

Jefferson children in droves up and down the gray street. Newspapers blowing, candy wrapppers from school parties, and beer cans in the gutter, few signs of Christmas. Cops swinging sticks or standing back on every corner, taut, unsmiling. Cars honking. Teen-agers in groups of eight and ten. They won't get off the street. Drunks come lurching through the gangs, which stand back, laughing loudly up at the windows.

Monty and Vernon leave the building with me. Monty smuggles a package into my hand, a handkerchief wrapped with a bow. He had carried groceries Saturday for the money. He said, "That bow cost an extra quarter, but you can use it later for your hair." I gave him a thank-you kiss on the cheek, and Vernon burst out laughing. Monty was very upset and did not speak again for an hour. He said, "White peoples aren't supposed to kiss colored peoples."

We are going to Curtis's house. We pass children eating penny candy, just standing on steps, looking out at nothing. When they get too cold, they'll go in the building and warm up. Then out and stand again. Eat some more candy. Four kids are smashing bricks ends from a building under demolition. Then more kids standing.

Curtis's mother's husband answers the door, a young man who Curtis said gets work at night, not often. His face is tense but expressionless. "No, he ain' here now; he's sick. She took him downtown."

As he is saying this, Curtis's mother appears around the door, leaning a little. She's been drinking heavily and covers her mouth with one hand. With the other she combs the back of her head.

"After New Year, is Curtis coming back to school? I don't want to see him suspended. But he's lost if he doesn't get back."

She can't focus. "Currie warn't in school?" she repeats several times. "Wul, I don' know what to do 'bout that boy. I wish he be in school, but he jus' gettin worse an' worse.

170

. . . Maybe I sen' him south awhile; he get tamed down there. . . . Warn't in school? Well, he s'pose to be in school; we sen' him out there today, didn' come? Always been *so* bad. . . . I don' know what to do about that hooky playin' an' all."

After Christmas

Curtis does not come back, but Vernon and Monty say he didn't go south either. "He jus' sittin there." Further, he was there the whole time that day. Monty: "Pokin his head aroun' behin' that door. I seen him, Laughhin!"

The first days of January the two boys play and replay the scene in Curtis's hallway.

MONTY.   First he father come to the door and say, "No, ain' here today, he sick. Wul no, my wife hadda take him some-where; he sick, not here now." Then Curtis' mother pop her ol' head aroun' the do' and he was pretty surprised, but he made no min' he lie!

And she look, and hol' her han' like this (forms fan of fingers over his mouth), and then a li'l baby sister come into that door. And the mother do this (fans) and baby do this (bends knees, beams upward, tipples a baby's bottle). And she say, "Wha' . . . Currie not bein guh'ddd?"

JOSIE.   Don't forget 'bout that chil' bein naked.

VERNON.   Wai', man, don' forget the thirty-dollar part.

MONTY.   There's not a thing I don't recall about it. She say, "Tuk thirty dollars off my purse, that were a week ago. An' Missus Dobbs, he nev' did come back with all that stuff she sen' him for. Nobody this block trusts that boy no mo'."

RICHARD.   She always hold her glass like that.

MONTY.   "Currie not doin the rah't thing in schoo'?" (Bursts out laughing.)

VERNON.   Pokin that stick through that ol' hair alla time.

MONTY.   That a comb. Pokin a comb through her hair.

VERNON.   Poke *her* hair, then she poke baby's hair. That ol' baby come out and (imitates baby, staggering forward, pencil in lips for bottle) look upppp . . . and down! . . . "Wha' . . . Currie not guh'ddd?" And that baby had no underpants on.

171

MONTY. And you know what happen to Curtis the day after Christmas? He is maaad! His friend Nemmie come by to see their Christmas tree and stole Curtis's new shoes.

The class soon forgets about Curtis, but other things begin to change. William and Roger make some handsome fish to hang around the bow of a Viking ship (a mobile), in January. New books are promised. Meanwhile, back to *Eagle*. Harold rereads how Eagle loads the arrow.

LEANORE. Eagle better watch that arrow, boy; it'll pop right back in his eye, and his eye'll pop out, and he'll have to go to the 'mergency ward of Mount Sinai Hospital, and the young intern'll have to put a cold compress on, or else *remove the entire eye.* You can give your eyes to science if you want. Nat King Cole did. Yes, Nat King Cole is dead. With his beautiful marcelled hair.

She is angry because other children have taken to reading *Madeleine.* Ernie is living with his grandmother and is ill, but his little sister came in for the book. "He want that Maddie and no other." Richard and Virgil now know half of the poem, and most children know the first two lines:

> In an old house in Paris, covered with vines,
> Lived twelve little girls in two straight lines.

What Leanore does is to start the next book, *Madeleine and the Gypsies.*

LEANORE. Madeleine better watch out the gypsies; they'll tell her fortune but steal her wallet. They do know many things that bring you good luck, except when the moon is full. The things that happen in my house in the full moon! Every full moon there's been a letter for us. Someone dropping dead on the street or in the subway, and my uncle out in Texas. I sure like that dress, is that the one cost thirty dollars?

TEACHER. Please don't poke me in the eye.

LEANORE. What do you think of this dress? A very rich kid wore it. There isn't a dress I wear for dress-up she wouldn't wear for play; that's how classy she is. But whatever I have to wear, it's always in beautiful condition. When a certain person burned our house down we were poor for a while. I had only one skirt. (Pause.) No. Three. But every single night my mother washed or ironed that skirt. That's my point, the *condition* of clothes. And to have matching jewelry, like Mrs. Weiss. I'd only wear rubies, like Mrs.

172

Weiss. But her jewels always match; jewels have to match perfectly.

TEACHER. Oh, I don't suppose they *have* to.

LEANORE. Yes, but it's in much better taste.

Another change is that Donald, advised by Mr. Ferré, has started fighting back.

RICHARD. I seen him yesterday, settin in Mr. Saltz' office and there was a big egg on the front of his head.

MALCOLM. His face was all funny colors, shiny pancake. Part of it green.

JOSIE. Teacher, can Donald get a job with his reading?

LEANORE. Oh, there's a job for Donald, I'm sure there is. He has *nice* eyes, nothing wrong with his eyes; but someone in his home don't care about him. If they don't, they should send him to the foster home. He'd be the nicest boy you'd ever want to find. I saw his mother go into the liquor store with high heels and nylons on Saturday, nothing wrong with the way *she* looked. She was gettin a bottle of Seagrams and you know what Seagrams is, five ninety-five a quart.

CASSANDRA. Miss Buh'ke, me and Iris we're goan get us a place when we grows up, and neither of us goan drop out of school. And we goan get us a house and a job, and share the money. We might be workers on a typewriter.

RICHARD. Instead of a drummer I wanta go in the Peace Corps, my minister said about, give the people who never ate an egg one. And a lotta people in China and India who don't have tooths.

The children know things about the civil rights movement now that they have learned outside as well as in school.

RICHARD. I bet if anybody get his head busted down there, Martin Luther King will fix that head because *he is a doctor.* I'd be proud to have him for a father.
—They don't know where he'll show up, in jail or out. He goes in that jail, slip out. Show up somewhere else. I like to be him, everybody loves him.

RUBY. He cried when he got the Nobel Peace. And his father and his whole family was proud of him. And his wife had to speak softly, she was so proud. She took a deep breath, she was thinking how he never forgot to give a compliment.

173

CASSANDRA. His sister say, he made all the difference to her life.

RUBY. And he loves everybody, even the whites people. He wants everybody to get mixed up together, the white and Chinese people and all. And he wants them to roller skate together and drink from the same drinking fountain, and not make fun of each other. They better not beat him again, or his wife won't sing any more.

JOSIE. He so good, I think he be from heaven.

VIRGIL. Once when we had Pres'dent Kennedy, Martin Luthern King was in jail, and the President had his brother call up person-ally (picks up telephone) and say, "You let him out of that jail; we need him; he is an important man."

(Other children are also picking up telephones, saying, "Hello, this is the White House.")

Say, I'm calling from the White House. We can't do without Martin Luthern.

TEACHER. Yes, but remember, he also has had to go to jail and be beaten up, not because he's hurt anyone or been bad but—?

MONTY. Miss Rosa Parks, her feet hurt. She wanted to sit in that ol' bus, but the driver said, "Please go to the back; you are a Negro." She said, "No, I don't have to go to that back so long's I paid my fare and ain't doin harm."

(Grumbling, angry currents start, as whenever the Parks incident has been mentioned. It seems to be more meaningful than events of later times.)

REGGIE. Oh, they wouldn' make me do that; boy, I punch anyone say that.

VIRGIL. But Martin Luthern say the person who punches ain't too intelligent. Ain't got it upstairs.

REGGIE. Listen, I punch anyone didn' give me a seat.

A later day. The Alabama voter registration drive. Earlier in the year the children had grown fond of the Norman Rockwell painting of the FBI leading a Negro child into the Little Rock school. I would like to remove this picture, but the children will not part with it. Now it is hard to separate the actions of Martin Luther King today from the earlier period.

CHILDREN. Did he get her in today?

174

TEACHER. No, that child did get into the school; that's all past. In Alabama they are now trying to get the right to vote. The whole world is with Martin Luther King down there.

WILLIAM. He'll get that chil' in; he'll take care of her.

MONTY. He is more better than Johnny Mathis.

MALCOLM. But don't say he is a movie star.

CHILDREN. That's right. Don't ever say that again.

(The children are to watch television of the voter registration drive for homework.)

REGGIE. I watches it on television; I told my mother it was homework and says, "Excuse me, Mother, may I switch to another channel? I wants to watch Martin Luthern King."

(Others copy this: "So did I; I say, 'Excuse me, Mother, but I needs to watch TV.' ")

CASSANDRA. I had that march on television; I say our teacher give it for homework, and he just turn it off. I ain't even look at him. He want to watch wrestlin. And I really be likin that picture of the people trying to vote, but he just turn it; say he don' care—he pay for this set; it's his set; he gonna watch what he please. I tell you one thing, though. He's not my real father.

MONTY. They all held up their hands—

(He does the state police of Alabama. William blows a whistle.)

Stop, everyone! Stop here!

CHILDREN. Now we gotta make a prayer.

VERNON. Step back, everyone; step back. Here is Martin Luther King.

CLAUDE. Someone tryin to punch the eyes outa the woh'den down theah. Those po-lice, they weah two colahs of blewww, down theah.

REGGIE. Never mind; Martin Luther King is there. He is there and three hundred Negros are there.

MONTY. Three hundred po-lice.

RICHARD. Huh, yeah, huh. (Muttering, jealous because he didn't see TV.) They better not tell *me* I wouldn' walk over no bridge.

I asked them to close their eyes and think about Martin Luther King for a minute today, the start of the Montgomery march.

REGGIE. What I thought about, I hope he be brave if anybody spits on him.

RICHARD. He went to Sweden and Norway and talked to the king. They gave him the Nobel Peace Prize. And they didn't care that he was another color. The Queen of Sweden wanted him to go right on talking, because he knew a lot of things she didn't know. They gave him a big dinner, there was a big band, it went on *real* late at night, and he just went on talking and talking to the king.

And they both had cutaway coats on.